YOU MAY BE GOOD AT SOMETHING

an autobiography

by

A. J. BILL BAILEY

YOU MAY BE GOOD AT SOMETHING

an autobiography by

A. J. Bill Bailey

"Sit down Bailey. You may be good at something but we've yet to find out what it is, it's certainly not Latin."
Latin master's comment 1942.

Published 2015
by Jill Tompkins Bailey
Berkswell, UK

C Copyright 2015 All rights reserved

ISBN 978-0-9927866-1-8

No part of this publication may be reproduced, stored, or made available in any form without prior approval of the author. Short extracts may how ever be used by individuals for their own purposes giving acknowledgment to the source.

Printed by
IngramSpark

Contents

PART ONE: EARLY DAYS 1928-1945

Chapter 1   Nought to Ten……………………….…..7

Chapter 2   Ten to Sixteen……………………..……22

PART TWO: ENGINEERING CAREER 1945-2001

Chapter 3   The Apprentice, Power Jets……………52

Chapter 4   The Austin Motor Company 1951-53….63

Chapter 5   Alvis Aero Engines 1953-63…………. 69

Chapter 6   Massey Ferguson 1963-88………...……95

PART THREE: LIFE 1945-2015

Chapter 7   Boating, Shooting, Cycle Racing…….111

Chapter 8   Family Life…………………………136

Chapter 9   Mountains……………………….149

Chapter 10   Summer Expeditions………..……..182

PART ONE

EARLY DAYS

1928 -1945

CHAPTER 1

Nought to Ten

December twelfth 1928 was a very important date for my mother. I was born. There were icicles a foot long outside the window, according to my mother. When she saw me my mother is reputed to have said "I don't think we'll rear him." I hope she meant it would be difficult to rear me rather than don't bother. I must have been a surprise because I already had a sister who was 6 years older than me.

I was christened Alfred John, a curse that was to stay with me all my life. The Alfred after one grandfather and the initials of the other. No one ever called me Alfred. My family called me John and the rest of the world called me Bill. It seems that most Bailey boys were called Bill after the song "Won't you come home Bill Bailey."

We lived at 70 York Street, Rugby, which was a dead end except for a footpath. The house was terraced with a shared back entry, no upstairs toilet or bathroom. We relied on "po's" (short for pot) for night time requirements. There was one coal fire in the lounge and another in the kitchen to heat the copper. The copper being a built in tub with a fire underneath which was lit early on Mondays, the ritual washing day when the kitchen was filled with steam. The washing was dried of course by pegging it on a line in the small back garden where the neighbours would compete for the whitest wash. Cooking was with a gas stove and a favourite method of ending it all at this time was putting one's head in the gas oven.

Women did not normally go out to work. There simply was not sufficient time. Shopping was a daily occurrence which meant walking in to town, no fridges, no cleaning aids, no central heating. Beds were warmed by stone hot water bottles. To prevent chilblains when walking on the cold lino floors we would wear hand knitted bed socks. A psychological study might, of course, show that we were just as happy then as today.

What do I remember? I had a second hand red pedal car and would hurtle down the pavement outside the house. One day I was pushed home semi conscious by two boys one of whom said I had been hit on the head by a bottle. The other said I had crashed. We never did establish the truth. The doctor who came lit a match a put it in front of my eyes and pronounced that I was not dead.

It was at this stage that I had identified my future career. Road sweeper. Once a week a gentleman would sweep the road pushing a barrow with iron wheels and I would rush in the house get my own broom and join him. Horses were used extensively for the delivery of bread, milk etc. because they would know the road and avoid getting in and out of vans as we do today. The by product of this system was steaming piles of horse muck which was eagerly shovelled up by entrepreneurial children who would sell it to residents for 1d a load. Horse manure was reputed to be exceptionally good for roses. All the houses had small front gardens full of flowers. Sometimes it was a race between residents and children who got to the steaming gold first.

My father would walk to his place of employment BTH where he was toolmaker. One hot day my mother dressed me in a smart outfit with a white shirt and said wait for your Dad at the bottom of the street. There I became entranced by the rivulets of melting tar which could be diverted and shaped with the aid of a small stick. By the time my father had arrived the tar was on me and little was left on the road. When we arrived home my mother kept shouting "just look at him" but my father who was never upset just laughed, which infuriated my mother even further. His attitude influenced me in later life – only bother about things you can do something about, the rest is history.

Another incident was the day my mother asked my sister to warm the butter in front of the fire so that it could be spread on the bread. The inevitable happened: the butter melted, slid off the plate and there was a great roaring inferno with an ensuing panic. What joy!

The next phase of my life was Chapel Street mixed school. The only things I recall were high windows with jars of dead flowers in them and big black dots illustrating the numbers 1 to 10. This is all I remember of that year.

After one or two years it was decided that I should go to Elborow boys' school where my father had been many years before. This Victorian school was a few minutes walk from home and had a catchment area from some of the tougher parts of town. The school was heated by large coke fires in the class rooms which meant you were roasted in the front of the class or frozen at the back. This wasn't the only problem. There was one boy by the name of Watts known as Wattie whose clothes and self had never been washed in his life. He always sat near the front of the class and smelt dreadfully. His nick name, Gasser Watts was fully justified.

The cane was used extensively and you were whacked on the hand by the teacher wielding a ruler. A Miss Sleath who was a keen tennis player had a fearful reputation. The only other thing I recall about this part of my education was that a teacher complained that when books were returned mine had little figures drawn around the edges. I must have learned something but I am not sure what.

An annual event was the visit of the photographer. My mother said whatever you do keep your mouth shut – see photo. My mother's reply when I requested boots instead of shoes was what do you want boots for? I explained that boots were good for kicking and that shoes put you at a disadvantage. I never did get boots!

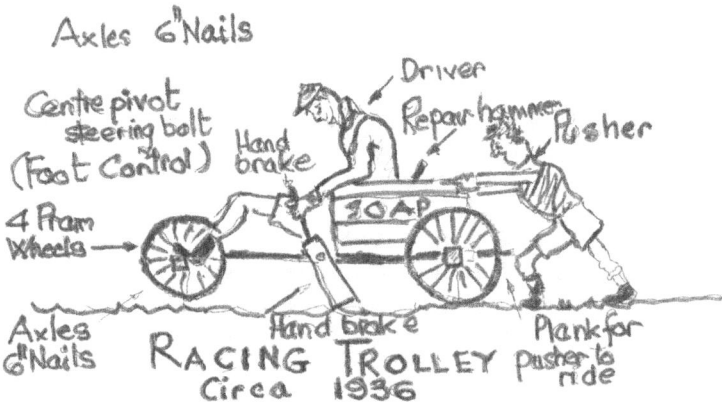

The street was safe from traffic and therefore was one big play area and virtually an extension to the home. Children were always playing in the street and you did not go to each others houses. There were crazes – marbles where you competed in such games as "nearest the wall" and "nearest the middle" of a chalked circle on the ground. An unsophisticated type of bowls, you had a little bag in which you carried your marbles and sometimes played for keeps which could result in a disaster – no marbles unless you could raise a half penny or better still a penny to buy some more.

The street was lit by gaslight and a gentleman by the name of Cleaver would come around on a bicycle with a long pole to which there was a device to light the lamps in the evening. He would come around in the morning to put them off. If anybody threw a stone and broke the glass then Mr Cleaver would be looking for them with a threat of physical retribution. It was not uncommon for us to have a spy in our midst so he in turn could be subject to physical violence. You were always a little dependent on your own fighting prowess. I was not that tough physically and had to rely on my wits and ability to run at high speed.

There were other games that were played in the street. Football, racing old tyres down the street, cap guns, catapults and spinning tops. A highlight was the conker season. We put a piece of string through a hole in the conkers we collected from under the chestnut trees. One boy held his conker aloft whilst the other swung his in an attempt to shatter the hanging conker. The procedure was then reversed and this continued until one of the conkers broke. Some boys carefully stored conkers from the previous year. These conkers had hardened and shattered the new ones. It was with great pride that you said you had a sixer which meant that you had seen off six other conkers. Claims were of course exaggerated but if somebody claimed to have a sixer or more and you saw it off then the glory was even greater.

Other entertainments included ditch jumping in the field at the bottom of the road. This involved jumping the ditch and going to wider parts until it became impossible and one fell in. There were so many things that one could do, even summer thunder storms could be exploited. After a down pour the sun would emerge and we would also emerge to dam the fast flowing rivulets with grass and soil to create mini lakes. Many an unsuspecting pedestrian would come around the corner to find a lake where the foot path used to be. Despite our best efforts to retain the flood water it would soon disappear and we would be off again to find other entertainments.

DITCH JUMPING

Trolleys were a favourite. These you built yourself out of bits of wood and old pram wheels. Good boxes and wood were highly sought after. Many a good lady with an older pram (and baby) was approached politely to ask if they could have the pram when she was finished with it. I was good at designing and making trolleys, an indication of inventiveness.

One of our pastimes was to visit a railway level crossing

close to home and put a half penny on the line to be flattened by a passing goods train. It was hoped that one could foil an unsuspecting shop keeper that it was a worn penny. Double your money!

A sport which was seasonal was wasp swatting. One of my friends whose father had a transport business had a

tip in the corner of his yard where rotten fruit was thrown. This would attract thousands of wasps and the sound of their buzzing could be heard yards away. There were generally three of us in the swatting team. We would first prepare ourselves – perhaps a balaclava hat, scarves etcetera and suitable attack weapons such as old cricket bats or tennis rackets were acquired for the offensive. We would leap into the corner for the battle; there were two hazards, the first being stung by a wasp the second being hit by another member of the team. First aid would nearly always be necessary at the end of the foray. Either sticking plaster for wounds or a blue bag applied to the wasp stings. The old fashioned remedy for stings was to put a blue bag, which was used for whitening washing, on the sting. I guess the blue bag was alkaline, but maybe a symbolic gesture.

Of course bonfire night was an exceptional occasion. Wood and rubbish were collected weeks before the event to make great bonfires. "Guys" (replicas of Guy Fawkes) were made out of old clothing. These guys were placed on foot paths or in wheel barrows and the makers would beg from passers by pleading "penny for the guy" which would be used to purchase fireworks. On November the fifth he was placed on top of the bonfire.

It was at this time, around 1938, a small red sports car would visit our house and take my father to work. It was only years later I realised it was Frank Whittle, the inventor of the jet engine, in the red car taking my father to Lutterworth to work on this highly secret project. I do remember my father being given a hundred Player cigarettes at Christmas. I got the box.

Sometimes we visited the Willens Works' sports grounds which was readily accessible from the bottom of our street. The ground's man, a Mr Downs, affectionately known as Downie, would chase us from his beloved grounds and you risked getting a clout on the ear if he caught you. We could escape by getting through some vertical railings which were wide enough for us to squeeze through but not for him. One day he must have bent a rail which allowed him access and I had a very near miss. There was a time he threw a stick at me which I picked up before making the security of the railings. Hero for a day.

One remarkable triumph of organisation and cunning was to collect a supply of old tyres and oil drums. Anything that would roll. The sides of the sports ground were steeply banked grass to allow for spectators at cricket matches. We carefully stored our weapons at strategic points around the ground, recruited a team of willing helpers and at appointed time shouted "Downie". When he rushed out of his pavilion we all rolled our tyres, drums etcetera down the banks. I had great respect for Downie, a true sportsman who metered out physical punishment liberally and provided us with a great challenge in our early years.

A time consuming hobby was the building of dens in the unkempt hedgerows in the fields around us. Dens were made by finding a suitable place in a thick hedgerow and tunnelling inside, the entrance being carefully hidden. We would line the den with hay and set about collecting sticks and piles of stones to defend ourselves against the raid of rival gangs. There was never a raid by a rival gang. Possibly another gang would build their den a few fields away and was sitting it out waiting for us? It was in the dens we tried smoking. You could purchase five woodbines in a paper packet for 1d. I never took up smoking but the experiment was illicit and exciting.

Once a week a special treat was a trip to the Regal Cinema for the children's matinee on Saturday afternoons. Here we could see films on Laurel and Hardy, Tom Mix the Cowboy, Tarzan and other stars.....Jean Autrey the Cowboy although he kept singing and I did not think much of this. The seats downstairs were 3d and upstairs 4d. If you could raise 4d there was a considerable advantage. You could hurl your empty or better still your almost empty ice cream tub on to the frustrated crowd below. The noise was deafening. Inspired by the films we would play in the woods Tarzan, Robin Hood, Pirates, Highwaymen, Captain Blood, all involving climbing trees and shouting at the top of our voices. If we could raise the necessary finance we would re-enact cowboy scenes using cap guns for a realistic effect.

We would visit the River Avon with family and friends equipped with a net, jam jar, sandwiches and a Thermos flask. We would then paddle in the river in the shallows below a small weir. This was known as Tom Brown's Island. The river was full of sticklebacks, bull heads and other water life including leaches. Leaches would occasionally attach themselves to an ankle and cause a drama and understandable consternation to the victim but great joy to the onlookers.

My mother thought it would be a good idea if I had piano lessons. A note from my music teacher confirmed my feelings that it was a waste of money. That together with the time that I left my music case hanging on railings while I went climbing trees was the end of my musical career.

Possibly the biggest event of the year was a trip to Eastbourne to visit my mother's parents for at least a fortnight. My father would be left at home to fend for himself. This was a bucket and spade holiday - ice cream on the beach, paddling in the sea. My grandparents lived on Firle Road, easy walking distance from the sea. The house was lit by gas as my grandfather Alf was the engine driver moving coal from the main line to the gas works. His engine was his pride and joy. He had a huge picture of his railway engines in the hall of his house, presented to him by the engine manufacturers. He would cook his breakfast of bacon and eggs on a polished shovel over the engine fire. If my grandfather came to the beach he would demonstrate how to dig oneself in....he claimed it was how he had survived the great war. Imagine me, the only child on the beach digging slit trenches while other children were making sand castles.

Eastbourne was famous for its piers and I was allowed to go to the pier on my own whilst my mother was on the beach. During my stay at Eastbourne I had amassed the princely sum of sixpence, all in halfpenny bits which I was determined to capitalize on. Along the length of the pier were slot machines. The machine I selected was one where you flicked a lever which sent a ball bearing flying and if it went down the right tunnel you got your money back and another go. I selected a machine and at the first go won. There was a clatter and half pennies began to pop down the chute. The machine had gone wrong. I looked around , there was nobody around. I filled my jacket pocket but could not pick the coins up fast enough. Coins were actually falling through the back of the pier in to the sea. Eventually the machine stopped, I guess it was empty, and I picked up the remaining coins. Looking around there was nobody to be seen and I decided to make a speedy exit. At the entrance to the pier was a man with a peaked cap. I walked past him conscious of the weight of coins in my bulging jacket pocked but he just smiled so I smiled back. I was free and rich. I spent the rest of the day counting the halfpennies and I was able to swap them for a silver half-crown at the corner shop. The half crown was sufficient to purchase a splendid cap gun that enabled me to re-enact the westerns we saw at the Regal cinema with great realism.

I was in Eastbourne aged ten when war was declared in 1939. It was not clear to me then what all the panic was about.

CHAPTER 2

Ten to Sixteen

1939, big changes! England declared war on Germany for invading Poland and that was the beginning of World War II. We were on holiday at Eastbourne at the time and I recall my mother saying that we would have to return to Eastbourne to avoid the bombing of the industrial Midlands. How wrong she was. The south coast was a target for German hit and run raiders and although we were bombed in Rugby the situation was worse in Eastbourne. We had a constant stream of people from Eastbourne avoiding the bombing and my grandparents lived with us for a great deal of the war.

When we returned from Eastbourne we went to a small general provision shop around the corner where there was a great heap of gas masks. The shop owner had been in the navy in the first world war and was a volunteer ARP man. He allocated the gas masks, which were in a simple cardboard box supported by a piece of string to carry the mask around your neck. Later people had better carriers as the boxes fell apart; and the masks had additional filters fitted, I guess to take care of another type of gas. You had to carry your gas mask everywhere and would not be allowed in cinemas, school, etc. without one.

The next event was the arrival of the evacuees. Small bewildered children from London were virtually dumped at the end of the roads, including ours, theoretically to escape the bombing of London. They had a small parcel of clothing and a label attached to them saying who they were and their London address.

There was no excuse, organisers went from house to house and you had to take one. My mother had already taken a policeman who was billeted on us so we were up to capacity. The evacuees were however moved on after a short time when it became evident that the industrial midlands, especially Coventry, were targets for the Luftwaffe. The policeman we had billeted with us went in to the army and quickly became an officer. When on leave he always took me rabbiting with him and introduced me to shooting.

Later my grandparents came up from Eastbourne to live with us. They had my room and I slept in the same room as my parents. My grandfather would take me walking – or did I take him? He was very knowledgeable about wild life, knew how to catch birds and find wild birds' eggs and we spent many happy hours in the countryside.

After a while, because of the continuous heavy air raids including the bombing of Coventry, my grandparents decided they would be no worse off if they returned to Eastbourne with its occasional hit and run raiders from across the channel. On their return they were provided with a Morrison shelter. The Morrison shelter, named after an MP, was of heavy steel construction with a steel top and heavy mesh sides. This was to be placed in the house to serve as a table (possibly a dining table with a cloth); you could readily dive in to it at short notice.

Alcohol was virtually unobtainable for civilians during the war and my grandfather decided he would use some of the precious sugar allowance to make some marrow rum. One day there was a tremendous explosion and my grandparents dived in to the Morrison. No siren, no all clear, they eventually emerged from the Morrison to find that my grandfather had put his mixture in to a stone screw top jar that had exploded. My grandfather was not allowed any more sugar for future alcoholic experiments.

I recall our teacher saying we should practice using our gas masks. I was subversively practising one day; the gas mask made a farting noise when you breathed out and my mother walked in to the room. She was very angry and said, "take it off. I don't care, you're not wearing that thing in the house." So much for the posters which said "Be Prepared". A further gas mask incident was that I left my mask at school by accident on one winter's evening. The siren sounded and when my father came in to work about eight pm. My mother was frantic. She said, "He's left his gas mask at school." "Never mind," replied my father, "he can have mine." Mother said "and what are you going to do". "I'll hold my breath was his answer." That diffused the situation, and there was never a gas attack. Far more deadly weapons were to emerge during the war.

The other major event was that I went to grammar School, the Lawrence Sheriff also known as "the Lower" being associated with Rugby school, the well known public school. If your parents could afford it there were scholarships for town boys from "the Lower" in to Rugby school, but extras such as uniforms, equipment, books were prohibitively expensive.

The reason I went to the "Lower" at ten was that my sister had passed the scholarship to the Rugby High School which had a capacity for 600 girls. My parents understandably did not want me to take the scholarship at 11 and fail to get a place in the boy's school of 400 which only took around 90 boys a year, one third of which would be scholarship boys. By entering the pre scholarship Form 2. I had only to appear reasonably intelligent to pass an entrance exam to be firmly ensconced in the "Lower".

When I went to the Lower in Form 2 many of the boys had already been there a year having been in Form 1 and were pals. For no reason whatsoever, three of the established lads leapt on me one lunch time and the fight ensued. Fortunately another boy in the class joined me, so it was three against two. Long ago at the Elborow school I had learnt that if you could draw blood then the opponents quickly collapsed. I managed a good smack on one of my opponent's noses and he rapidly disappeared bleeding from the fray. We were triumphant! My fighting partner remained a friend throughout my school days. I never had to seriously defend myself again, my reputation was sufficient.

I have always been eternally grateful to my parents for their decision to send me to the Lower. It taught me the

Victorian ethic of work or suffer the consequences. I was not a bright pupil but I am still surprised in later life how much I learnt by punishment and discipline.

The first day at the Lower school was intimidating. Lots of big boys with books under their arms whilst the new boys were assembled in the Big School. Here we sat apprehensively on benches at ancient battered desks. The desks were covered in carved initials of previous students. It was here that we were issued with wooden pens and "the school nib". This nib was standard issue and you were only given one and it was the only nib you were allowed to use. If you damaged or lost your nib a new one could be issued for a half-penny. Ink monitors were also appointed whose job it was to ensure that all desk ink wells were full at the beginning of class. I should mention at this point that carving one's initials on desks was forbidden. Later, some devious enemy of mine carved my initials on a desk, for which I was caned. I am still looking for the swine who did this!

The punishments were many and varied. First of all there was copy. This involved copying the top line of copper plate writing on the dozen or so lines below. Typical top lines were "I must not talk in class". You could be handed several sheets of copy for minor misdemeanour's and if the writing was not good enough you had to repeat the exercise. The cane was administered only by the head master. Three strokes across the back side for minor offences and a scale of up to six for more serious offences . The head master had a selection of canes of varying effectiveness. For a very serious offence you could be given six, sent to run around the field and given six more. You carried the marks and they were often zebras in the showers after physical training.

Legend has it that a new master asked the head why he only dealt with caning and should not give rewards for good performance. The head master said this was a good idea and a pupil was sent to the head for excellent work. Before the boy could explain to the head why he was there he was caned!

I clearly recall my first visit to the headmaster for caning. My misdemeanour was to open a door too fast when a master was on the other side holding a pile of books. Take this to the head, the master said, writing a quick note and sealing it. Off I went to the headmaster's study in the big house which was part of the school. On arrival there was a queue of boys standing in a green painted, spartan corridor. They were counting. One, two three....one two three four...or six ....boys would then emerge from the study grim faced and not stopping to chat. It was only when I was near the head of the queue and I could hear the impact of the cane, that I realised they were counting the number of strokes. My turn came. I went in to the study beautifully carpeted with book cases and a magnificent desk and a window which looked over the playing field. There stood Cordy with his robe and mortar board hat and one hand under his gown. Bend over, he said, and I had three strokes over my trousered back side. Obviously he had the cane hidden under his gown for easy access. Don't do it again, he said as I left the study.

The peculiar thing about being caned was that once the pain had subsided slightly you cheered up considerably and in many ways I preferred caning to detention. Grit your teeth and get it over with policy. Detention was on Saturday afternoons. We went to school Saturday morning so the loss of leisure time was a serious matter. You could opt for "caning out" - three strokes for one hour and four strokes for two hours. Although the extra stroke for the additional hour does not seem much it was administered across the existing strokes and was pretty painful.

Yet another insidious punishment was monitors detention. This was a system where monitors from the sixth form, lads of sixteen or seventeen, could give you black marks for minor offences, such as running between classrooms, stepping on the quadrangle grass, or forgetting your hymn book. When you had accumulated three black marks you had to stay in after school on a Friday night and do "civil service tots". These "tots" were contained in small books, each page having twenty figures across and about fifty down. If you got one right, the monitors, (the monitors had an answer book), you could go. I never did get one right and neither did anyone else. They let you go after one hour, mentally drained. In the five years I was there we only had one suicide, which is a bit surprising.

One other system of discipline was the daily report. This was an arrangement when you were given a small paper book and a blank space for each lesson. The appropriate master filled in comments. The book had to be counter signed by the parents each day and you had to turn up at eight every morning for the head master to look at the book. School started at eight thirty. If you had bad daily reports you would be subjected to other punishments, the ultimate being expulsion from the school.

You could be punished for not having your hat on straight, forgetting your gas mask, walking in town more than two abreast, for eating or drinking in the street, for opening doors quickly. I had my first three strokes of the cane for opening a door too fast. You were not allowed to talk to girls in public. One interesting technique which I think the Japanese also used during world war II, if the culprit of a crime did not own up the whole class or group was punished. This seemed an effective way of sorting things out quickly.

Clothes were rationed during the war and you needed coupons for each item of clothing. When I started at the Lower my school cap was grey with a coloured band denoting my house. There were four houses, mine was Tait and had a splendid red band. As the war progressed the coloured school caps were no longer available and we could only get a plain blue hat for all houses. I needed a new hat, my original one had fallen apart and my mother purchased a new blue one for me using the precious clothing coupons. There was only one problem. The hat was enormous, there appeared to be only one size. Embarrassed by the hat I decided to shrink it whilst my mother was out. I subversively soaked the hat in water and hung it in front of our coal fire. Operations were interrupted by a knock on the door. It was one of my pals, calling to discuss fishing. I forgot the hat. Half an hour later I noticed a smell of burning and rushed back in to the dining room where the back of my hat was smoking and glowing in front of the fire. I panicked and quickly washed the hat but a substantial part of the back had gone. No choice, I had to confess to my mother. Never mind, she said, I'll darn it,, we have no more clothing coupons. Not only did I still have a big hat, but a darned one as well. I should have settled for a big hat.

During my five years at grammar school the head master was Cordelius Wheeler, known amongst the boys as Cordy. Cordy had been a colonel in the first world war and I think was decorated for gallantry. When the second world war was declared he was put in charge of the Home Guard in Rugby and the school was used for training purposes. He was over six foot and a frightening figure of a man. One day Cordy was demonstrating on the school field the technique of throwing hand grenades. One recruit made a very poor throw and Cordy said "not like that you fool", picked up the concrete grenade and hurled it a spectacular distance to hit the shoulder of a boy who was innocently walking past. The victim whose name I remember but will not disclose had a weak heart to add to the joy. The news of the event went round the school in seconds and there was much rejoicing..... "did you know that Cordy nearly killed x?"

Rugby was never heavily bombed but when Coventry was blitzed you could hear the bombing and the glow in the sky made it seem like day light. We did have one incendiary in our garden and thought perhaps we were in for heavy bombing because incendiaries were sent first to light the way for the bombers with high explosives. There was one incident about this time which had a profound effect on me.

Years previously, when at Elborow, we would follow a footpath that went past a cottage that had a fruit and vegetable garden. We discovered that by pushing our hands through the wire netting we could steal some enormous pink desert gooseberries – stealing fruit was known as scrumping. One day we were caught by the owner, a kindly elderly man by the name of Percival. He laughed at our thievery and apprehension and said why didn't we come through the gate and help ourselves. We respected his kindness and always liked the way he chatted to us and treated us as equals.

When the war began Mr Percival volunteered his services as an air raid warden and was in charge of an air raid shelter close by his cottage. We had one night of heavy bombing, both incendiaries and explosives across our street. The fact that we had been bombed most of the night was no excuse for not going to school. My mother said she had some sad news for me when I returned from school. Mr Percival had been killed while ushering the last person in to the shelter.

So what about learning? It was a traditional grammar school so we were taught Latin, German, French, English literature, English grammar, divinity, biology, physics, chemistry, maths and art or woodwork. I struggled at school because I was not good at learning by rote. A kindly English master whose nick name was Jack and had encouraged my running said to me "Come and see me after school." He said "Tell me why you won't learn Shakespeare?" I replied " Well sir my mind keeps wandering to other things." "Such as?" he asked. I explained that I was trying to catch a big pike which I knew lurked in a half filled tunnel of water off a mill pool, and the currents prevented me putting the bait in the best place. I had plans to use a balloon to carry the bait in the right direction but the wind had to be favourable. After careful thought he said "you're not a fool are you Bailey, to which I replied that I did not know. He said would I just learn a little Shakespeare, which I duly did. I can remember it now: "Once more unto the breach dear friends, once more…" prologue to Henry V. As I left the study he said "Let me know if you catch that pike." A true gentleman.

Two other bits of Shakespeare that I recall were "and hair like mouldy hay" being the description of Dick the Shepherd, and, "Methinks I smell horse piss" – a useful phrase to shout when a master was approaching a classroom.

The Latin master had a rather different approach. You were often told to stand up and translate from the text before you. When it was my turn the Latin master said "Sit down Bailey, you may be good at something but we have yet to find out what it is. It's certainly not Latin." I heard a few years later that he was walking around the town with premature Alzheimer's whilst I was pursuing a successful career as an engineer. You never know what is around the corner.

Some days at morning assembly in the big school if the organ master was absent a school boy took his place. Before the masters assembled he would stride up and put up three numbers for the appropriate hymns. Then he would sit at the organ and begin to play, demonstrating his prowess in an arrogant manner. What he did not know this day was that a boy had changed the numbers to "All things Bright and Beautiful." The masters came in to the hall and "the creep" started to play his selected tune and four hundred boys sang All Things Bright and Beautiful. Chaos…

Sport was an important part of school life and Tuesday and Thursday afternoons were dedicated to this. You could only evade sport by producing a death certificate which was a bit tough on those that disliked sport. Rugby in winter, cricket in summer and cross country running in spring. The whole school ran about five miles, setting off in groups. Depending on the time taken you were awarded points for your house on a nought to five scale, five being good. When I started at school two of the lads said "We know a short cut, come with us." I said OK and low and behold there was a master at the end of the short cut who said report to me at the next run. I duly did this and we started off, me running, him on his bike: "start trying, catch the one in front." Despite the pain I began to get the satisfaction of overtaking and I finished with a four. He said " Five next week" and I was hooked.

One great step forward was when I discovered I was being nobbled. On Tuesdays, the running day, my grandmother who lived with us made bacon pudding. A tiny bit of bacon wrapped in suet pudding. She said it would "do you good". She was obviously oblivious of the effect of suet pudding on a cross country runner. I looked forward to running and always did well at a mile or more.

One of my successes was to run against Rugby School in a steeple chase know as the Rainsbrook Run. Lots of brook jumping and mud. I was picked although I was possibly the youngest member of the school team. Again I owe a lot to the master who said "report to me".... I will never know why he picked on me rather than my two companions.

In addition to the long distance running we had running on the sports field. But I was never any good at the short distances however I excelled at the mile and over. My father promised me six pence for every race I won at school, a decision he was to regret but cheerfully paid up.

Although perhaps not the best climber in the school I always enjoyed the challenge of climbing. Our form room was on the second story and one of my pals challenged me to climb down using the slightly decorative brick work for foot and hand holds. I was half way down when I saw below the head master, no escape! Was he going to look up? Yes – when I ultimately reached the ground he said, "Don't do that again." There was no punishment, I do not know if it was admiration for risk taking or relief for me not falling. Remember lots of his ex pupils were being killed in the war, taking risks to save the nation. Perhaps he thought we needed people to take risks?

I was never much good at cricket and all I seemed to do was field, never getting a chance to bowl or bat. However there was an alternative and that was swimming and life saving classes. These classes were

normally held at the Rugby Municipal pool. Soon I got all my certificates and a bronze medal for life saving and by fifteen I was an instructor. One day I said to the master in charge of life saving that I thought practising in the swimming pool was useful but we needed lake and river experience. To my surprise he said OK go ahead. I quickly gathered together some tin cans with lids on them, punched one or two holes in the side and sank them in the river Avon where there was a current. What fun tracing the bubbles and retrieving the cans.......my class was always full, eight was the limit. I obtained a bronze medal instructors certificate the year I left.

Whilst not learning much about Latin or cricket I guess I did learn something about leadership and enthusing a team which was to be valuable in later life.

I went to school when the war began and finished when the war ended. Although the impact of the war was not felt initially the effects became evident after Dunkirk. Food was rationed, and most nights the siren sounded and we would crouch in a cupboard under the stairs. My mother would listen when the aircraft passed close by and she would say "Hark. Listen. What's that?"...and then "It's all right, it's one of ours." The German bomber engines were diesel and had a distinctive note.

Food was short during the war and the school provided boys to help with the potato harvest. We were paid five pence and hour but gave half to the Red Cross. Two hours of back breaking work enabled you to go to the cinema in the cheapest seats. Prices at the cinema were 4pence for the first 6 rows, and 6 pence for the rows at the back. My friend Stanley developed a plan where you bought a four-penny ticket which was torn in half as you entered the darkness of the cinema. The ticket half was then swapped for a half of a six-penny ticket found on a previous visit on an ash tray. The usherette, on examining the half ticket would show you to the 6 penny seat. Stanley always took a bag of carrots to the cinema for refreshment, sweets being unavailable. Whilst this was OK I was never clear why he had to put them in a brown paper bag. The rustling of brown paper and the crunching of carrots always ensured there was plenty of room around us.

Stanley's father at one time did have a bottle of whisky hidden away. More out of devilment than taste we would take a surreptitious swig then replace it with water. Unknown to us Stanley's brothers were doing the same, I think his dad was saving it for Christmas and he must have been somewhat disappointed. Shortage of drink led the The Cherry Tree pub near Rugby to raise a Union Jack when they had a barrel of beer available. Workers would down tools for a pint before it all disappeared.

When I was about fifteen a pal and myself were sent to a farm to help with the potato harvest . After the first visit we always volunteered quickly for work at that farm because we so much enjoyed wrestling with the land army girls in the hay barn at lunch times.

A profitable business for me was keeping tame rabbits for the table. You were allowed a special bran ration provided you took some rabbits to the local butcher. I would often have as many as twenty rabbits. I made my own hutches which were of an ingenious design and admired by many. I also ran an effective business sending the skins of the rabbits to a company who made them in to furry gloves. Because clothing was on coupons and you needed a few coupons for these rabbit skin gloves I had a long waiting list from my sister and her friends. Proceeds from my rabbit farming later contributed to the purchase of my first dog.

In the school holidays we were always busy. At the age of eleven one of my pals, "Butcher Clark" (being the son of a village butcher), said "let's go camping." Several of us got together and decided camping was the thing to do that summer. We borrowed a tent from the scouts which , being very heavy, we pushed on a cart and pitched it by the canal. The farmer, being a friend of Butcher Clark's father, was very helpful. We filled sacks with straw to sleep on and had blankets with big safety pins (no sleeping bags in those days). Cooking was over a wood fire.

My mother had said I could go in the day but not stop over night. I moaned so much that in desperation she said "clear off then". I went and it took them a fortnight to find me. She forgot to ask where I was going. I still remember fetching the milk from the farm and smelling bacon and eggs cooking over a wood fire a field away. We camped for five weeks. This was the first of many camping expeditions, all local.

I have another delightful memory of Butcher Clark. The English master said that for homework we had to write a

poem. The first lines were to be -
"I would live if I had my will "
When we duly assembled at the next English lesson I recall the dialogue as follows:

Master "read your poem Clark."
Clark "I would live if I had my will
          "In a caravan with Uncle Bill"
Master "Go on"
Clark   "That's it"
Master " What do you mean "that's it" ".
Clark " It's a very short poem."
Master "Two hours detention Saturday afternoon will give you time to write a somewhat longer poem."
For weeks afterwards when we saw Butcher Clark we would say "How's your Uncle Bill". I think Butcher Clark was the winner of the encounter.

While at school I had numerous hobbies. We used to swim in the river or swimming baths. One of the best places to swim was Newbold quarry where you could leap or dive off cliffs in to fifty feet of water. I always told my mother I was going to the open air swimming pool. In retrospect I was probably safer in the quarry than the swimming pool because polio was rife before the vaccine was developed.

One of my pals who was older than me had left school and had acquired a length of rubber tubing. His proposal was that we could make a diving outfit by attaching the tube to a gas mask and dive to great depths in Newbold quarry. The trials just below the surface were reasonably successful so I volunteered to hold a big rock in my hands while he held the tube above water in the deeper part of the quarry. I plummeted into the depths, dark and cold, but the inlet air suddenly stopped, the pipe had collapsed with the increasing water pressure. I dropped the rock and hurtled to the surface. My so called friend claimed I actually cleared the water. No more diving.

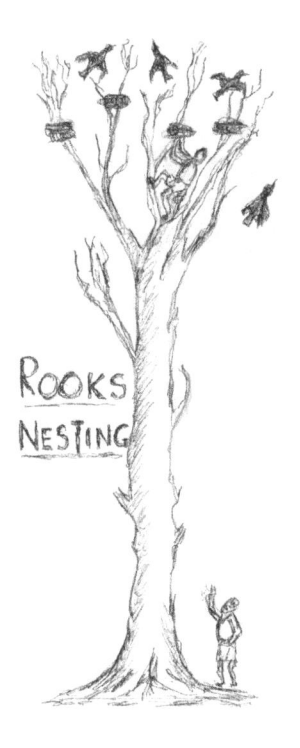

Other sports were rooks nesting, and moor hen nesting. The rooks nesting was a sport we undertook in the Easter holidays and involved climbing the large trees to the topmost branches and taking the rooks' eggs. The rooks eggs varied considerably in colour and the idea was to get a varied collection. The climbing was both hair raising and dangerous. The farmers did not mind as it kept the rook population under control. One lad was a spectacular climber and would leap from one branch to another sixty feet up. Not me.

The moor hen nesting was completely different. Nearly every field had a pond which supplied cattle water prior to piped water. In addition there were canals, rivers, and lakes all over the place. There were lots of moor hen nests in the spring – in the reeds, on fallen branches, anywhere that was difficult to get to. Moor hens lay up to ten eggs and we would risk falling in or at least getting a foot full of water to steal the eggs. The war was on, food was short, and moor hen eggs tasted good and provided an excellent meal. There were techniques for determining whether the eggs were fresh and not set.

When I was about fourteen I said to my Dad, can I have a dog. To my surprise he said yes. My pal Butcher Clark knew where there were some six week old liver and white springer spaniels for sale. They were at a relations farm at Easenhall near Rugby. They were ten shillings each and I had more than that in my National Savings book. I borrowed my sister's bike because it had a basket on the front and pedalled seven miles in the dark to purchase the furry bundle that was to become my pal for years to come. I could not wait for the weekend in case the pup was sold.

One great sport when the dog grew up was moorhen hunting in winter. The technique, for which the dog was essential, was to visit rivers, ponds and old canals. Moorhens dive under water frequently when being pursued but leave a trail of bubbles. Eventually they pop up at some hidden spot to take in air. The dog, or a well directed stone, or a shot with a catapult would make them dive again until exhausted they would come to the surface to be retrieved by the spaniel. Two or three moor hens made a welcome addition to the meagre rations, especially as we were short of protein foods. Later when I left school and obtained my first shotgun the spaniel became an essential partner flushing and retrieving rabbits and game.

Another place to swim was Little Lawford mill pool, a short cycle ride from home. A tree hung over the pool and we decided unanimously that it would be wonderful if we had a rope to swing out over the pool and let go. So we had to procure a rope. First we had to establish where to find a suitable rope,. We visited an ironmongers where a man in a brown gown pointed at a great coil of magnificent rope in the corner of the shop. How much would the required length of rope be? Five shillings we were told. We all gasped. It would take a month to raise that sum, but we were undeterred and set about raising the money. We visited the shop every week to look at the rope

The Rope

where the man confirmed as we walked through the door that he had plenty of rope and that they would not sell out. He did invite us to look at and admire the rope. Eventually, having run errands, returned empty pop bottles, and saved our pocket money, we arrived at the shop before it was open. The man in the cow gown arrived and said "come to look at the rope?" No we said proudly, we've come to buy it. We emptied our coins on the counter, sixpences, pennies and half-pennies, while the man measured the rope along the brass measure set on the edge of the counter.

A glorious summer day and we were off with the rope, it being carried proudly on the shoulder of one of the gang. We all had our bathers heading for Little Lawford mill.

No time was wasted and one of the lads climbed the tree, crept along a suitable branch and tied the rope. Who was going first? An eager volunteer walked back holding the rope, tore down the bank to swing out over the pool where he dropped gracefully into the water. Me next was the cry and we all took turns to swing out over the pool. We spent all day in the pool and until dusk fell and driven by fatigue and hunger it was time to go home. Catastrophe! The rope had tightened with constant use and was wet. We could not budge it. Should we cut it? We could not leave it! Eventually with the aid of an old piece of iron we were able to free it and we returned home, tired, hungry and happy. We took the rope with us many times but we were never quite able to repeat the excitement of that first day.

Despite the numerous punishments that threatened us while we were at school we were always devising pranks to break the monotony and rigid discipline. I recall one particularly successful plan. We had a fearsome maths master known as The Bull. He would leap in to the room throwing board rubbers and strike fear into the hapless pupils. He then always cleaned the blackboard fervently with a duster as if the board was an enemy.

I had a brilliant idea! I kept rabbits at the time and always had a casualty or two when the little furry creatures were a few weeks old. I wrapped a dead rabbit in the duster. The whole room went quiet when The Bull leapt in to the room and started to clean the board with the duster in which I had encased a small rabbit.

Suddenly aware of the squidgy feeling The Bull peered in to the duster. The silence was awful. Who did this? He said quietly. We noticed he had gone rather pale. Knowing of group retribution I owned up and expected to be sent to the head for a thrashing – but of course I would be the hero of the class. He then said very quietly he thought it was a clever plan because of his dislike for dead animals and we had identified his only weakness. There would be no retribution. The whole class clapped and his pupil to master relationship changed and we all learnt more maths as a result. I was a hero for a day and the story of The Bull and the rabbit went round the school in minutes.

I was always popular at school because amongst other things I knew about fishing. Because I was interested I read books, experimented and went to numerous fishing spots. School work poor, fishing prowess excellent. A fishing story that is worthy of mention is the tale of a visiting aunt who came to visit us from London. She was a superior type of person and had travelled a great deal and had a habit of talking down to people, especially me. I recall my mother had obtained, with great difficulty, a chicken for dinner. When my aunt arrived she said "I do hate the smell of cooking" whilst I was going crazy with the aroma that I had last smelt the previous Christmas.

However on the day my aunt arrived I was going fishing with a pal. We went down to the river Avon and fished under the river bank and caught a few small perch. Suddenly I hooked something enormous which headed to the centre of the pool. It was a great yellow eel. Eventually I got the eel to the steep bank where my friend, who had a landing net, netted it and we landed it on the bank. The great writhing eel fought free and slithered gracefully back in to the pool. We were both disappointed but elated. When I returned home for my lunch I excitedly told my story to all present including my aunt. Everybody was sympathetic except my aunt who said it was just a fisherman's story. Little did she know!

THE MONSTER EEL

That evening we returned to the river bank and unbelievably caught another eel. A lot smaller, possibly about two feet long, black and slimy. My pal said we should take it home because his dad liked eel to eat, so I put it in my fishing bag. I eventually went home a dusk and went in to our small dining room where the family, including my aunt were assembled. On arrival my aunt asked if I had any more fishing stories. I walked across to her, opened my bag, and pulled the eel out to show her. She screamed and went all peculiar and there was a great deal of consternation. My mother fetched some smelling salts. I went to bed that night tired and happy: my aunt left the following day.

Whilst not starving during the war, our diet was very limited, bread and potatoes being a significant part. As a result if we caught a fish, say a perch of half a pound, it would be a welcome contribution to a meal. At this time the river Avon was beautiful, clean and unpolluted. The river was full of gudgeon, small fish which we cursed and frequently threw back a bucket full while pursuing the bigger fish. Many years later I was travelling close to the Seine in France where I was served a delicious grilled fish dish. When I enquired what they were I was told "goujon", a quick look in the dictionary, gudgeon – if only we had known!

It was about this time, because I was fifteen, I applied to be a messenger boy for the civil defence organisation. You had to have a bike and you were given a smart beret and bag in which to put messages to the fire brigade, ARP etcetera if the phone lines were down. The air raid threat was reduced now except for V1 and V2 flying bombs and rockets which did not reach Rugby. I never did get my uniform as the war was coming to an end.
During the school holidays we made a contribution to the war effort by collecting scrap metal. We used to first of all visit a local undertaker to borrow his cart normally used for coffin transportation.

It would have been indiscreet to ask whether the coffins were full or empty when he used the cart but it proved to be an excellent way to convey scrap. Other teams collected scrap and we had a great pile of old saucepans, cast iron bedsteads etcetera. Eventually a lorry came to school and took it all away. It was said that it was to help build a Spitfire! I have my doubts.

Towards the end of my school days the war with Germany ended and the whole town celebrated in the streets. You could hardly move in the town square. My two pals who were older than me went in a pub and bought me a pint of bitter which I consumed outside and acquired a taste which has been with me all my life.

It was my final year at school and I went to the school harvest camp where we camped in an old orchard in bell tents and helped local farmers with the harvest. The masters and mistresses stopped in old stables and did the cooking. We soon established that if we climbed an old pear tree we could gaze in to an upper room window and watch the love making of one of our masters and a mistress. Unfortunately there was only room for two boys at a time on the branch so we had to take it in turns. We only had one or two mistresses at the school at the end of the war to replace the masters who had been called up or were doing war work.

We had one little adventure at harvest camp. We were all feeling quite bored. In the darkness it was suggested that we should go up the tower of a nearby church. Off we went, creeping through the churchyard. The church door was unlocked and we climbed the bell tower on to the roof. Having achieved our objective we went down and out in to the graveyard when somebody shouted "ghosts". There was a mad rush and we all ran in the darkness until we all lay breathless and laughing until a quiet voice said "where's bomber"? One of our number was missing. He was with us when we left the church someone said. We had one rather dim torch and we returned quietly and apprehensively in search of Bomber. On returning to the church yard we could vaguely hear a grunting sound and splashing. Slowly and fearfully we followed the sound. Bomber had fallen in to a newly dug grave and could not get out. He was covered in mud, breathless and wild eyed. It took a little time to quieten him down and clean him up. It was my last school day adventure.

While at harvest camp the war with Japan ended. We got on our bikes and rode the twelve miles to Rugby where the whole town was celebrating. Bands playing, dust bin lids banging and marching around the streets singing. I remember clearly four boys from the school pushing a piano around the streets while one of my school pals who was a talented pianist played it.

School was over, the war was over, what lay ahead for me?

PART TWO

AN ENGINEERING CAREER

1945 – 2004

CHAPTER 3

The Apprentice

Aged 16 to 21 at Power Jets

The war was over. I left school aged 16 with a rather poor school certificate. My father asked me what was I going to do and I replied that I wouldn't mind being a game keeper, or there was a job going at a timber merchants as a trainee surveyor. He said he did not wish to influence me but thought there was a job for me at Power Jets as an apprentice if I was interested.

I duly applied and was granted an interview. I put on my suit, washed and took the train to Whetstone near Leicester where I had an interview. I was told they did not have a formal scheme but the plan was they would send me to Leicester Technical College (now Leicester university) two days a week. The other three and a half days (including Saturday mornings) would be spent in the workshops and eventually the technical offices. If I proved capable I would become an engineer apprentice but if I did not succeed they would possibly offer me a trade apprenticeship - machinist, tool maker, pattern maker or other engineering crafts.

I received a formal offer for an apprenticeship from them by post. This meant I had get up at 6 to catch a bus at 6.45am from the centre of Rugby to start work at 7.30am. It was clearly a case of nepotism, influenced by my father's years working on Frank Whittle's jet engine. Somebody, possibly one of my father's contacts, took me through the main factory and then up a drive a quarter of a mile long to the test area. The noise of engines, compressors etc on test combined with the pervading smell of paraffin fuel was somewhat overwhelming. I was quickly taken to the foreman in the combustion test area who said right, you can work with Ted.

Gaining workshop experience at Power Jets

Ted looked at me and handed me a brown cow gown. No fancy inductions in those days. Ted was my mentor and said "Cut that length of piping into 6 inch pieces and handed me a hack saw." This I did the de-burring the ends and checking the lengths. He said "You've handled tools before" and seemed pleased to have me working with him. My experience of designing trolleys and making rabbit hutches started to pay off rather than the Latin.

I quickly established myself and learned how to solder, weld, braze and bend pipes etc to build test rigs to vague sketches. After about 2 months the foreman said I should work on my own to the technical engineers requirements. Soon I was helping the professional technical engineers doing tests and taking measurements. I heard indirectly that they had requested me to join them in the offices as a junior engineer and that I was wasted doing practical work. I moved for a short spell to the engine testing area where complete engines were tested. When I arrived the foreman said he had a very interesting job for me. I was elated until he explained that I would be throwing dead chickens into an engine intake to simulate a bird strike.

He explained I would be behind a steel screen but did not tell me that the chickens obtained from a nearby chicken farm were somewhat "mature". A lot of feathers, a strong smell but I joined in the laughter of the team in the insulated observation room and said I was looking forward to doing it again and nobody else should be considered for such a desirable job. A far better response than complaining and very well received by the team. I know the foreman and superintendent both gave me a very good report on my stay in the test area.

My next move was to the aero engine assembly to work with George, a very competent fitter. Here I learnt a great deal about the disciplines of aero engine assembly. You can kill a lot of people if you get it wrong!

A few days in to the new year of 1947 it started to snow and did not stop. It was not possible for me to get to work. At the time I did not realise how fortunate this was to prove. I had been struggling with my technical college work. I now had time – an unusual commodity! - so I went to a large book shop in Rugby and purchased with my savings some books. They were a Teach Yourself series and covered subjects such as mathematics, including calculus, mechanics, hydraulics, thermodynamics. I set myself up in the cold back bedroom determined to work 6 hours a day.

The bedroom had the advantage of having the hot water tank situated in it; the water tank was heated by a coke fire in the kitchen. The only way to get some coke was to take a sack and bicycle to the gas works through the snow where you could purchase one sack of coke per person. You then pushed the sack of coke on to the bike. I did this several times to the advantage of the family who sat by the fire in the kitchen. But it was at the expense of study time. I settled for being cold but educated. The books all had tests at the end of each chapter and I was able to monitor my progress. To my surprise I found not only did I understand the work but I actually enjoyed the tests. It gave me confidence, perhaps I was not so

daft after all!

Having spent several weeks disciplining myself to my studies, the company asked for volunteers for those who could return to work. Somebody had the bright idea that if we mounted some of the older jet engines on tanks and railway engines the heat and thrust would clear the snow. What fun, we cleared lines and roads that had been impassable.

Not only did we do the preparations on these engines but went in to action with the finished lash ups. One night after working all day our vehicle got stuck five miles from Rugby and two of us walked home through six foot drifts. It was dark and it was difficult to know where the road was.

It eventually thawed although there was still snow on the ground in May. On returning to college I found I was able to handle the work as a result of my studies during the deep freeze. An outstanding event for me was when one of my colleagues, who I had held in great esteem for his technical ability, asked me to help him with a particularly difficult question. My confidence hit a new level when I realised I was capable of becoming a chartered professional engineer.

More luck! Although the main works were at Whetstone near Leicester, Power Jets still retained the original test facilities at Lutterworth for teaching purposes. It was here that students from the UK, the Armed Forces and overseas were given courses on jet engines. There was a requirement for a versatile fitter to prepare engines. The fitter I had worked with on engine assembly suggested I would be a useful assistant. I could do this, go to lectures and take time off for studies. As well as the Power Jet engines, we also stripped a De Havilland Goblin and a Rolls Royce Derwent Five; we sectioned them prior to reassembling them as "cut away" engines showing all the inside workings.

After the war time restrictions the food on the site was marvellous. The chef said that he was not going to prepare special meals for us so we ate the same as the residents at nominal costs. At the end of each course the students and lecturers had a dinner at the Greyhound hotel in Lutterworth. Free beer and food – what a splendid time. I found it easier to cycle the eight miles from Rugby than to bus or train there. The four months at Lutterworth was wonderful experience.

The first Whittle Jet engine to fly

The next stage of my career was to move from the work shops in to the technical offices. The best route for this was through the jig and tool drawing office because you could get an introduction from the tool room foreman. There was no problem as I had acquitted myself well in the tool room. I duly went to see the chief draftsman who looked me over in my suit, tie, clean shirt, shining shoes, and said yes, he would have me in the office. "No talking or whistling! Bring me your first drawing."

I was put to work with a senior draftsman and in due course, very carefully, produced my first drawing. I thought it was quite good and took it to the chief draftsman. He promptly tore it up and said "do it again and bring it back to me." He looked at my second drawing and said "put it away and keep it." After four months I went to see the chief draftsman to tell him I was moving on. He was quite amiable and said "fetch your first drawing.....do you think you have learnt anything?" The difference between my latest drawing and the first one was remarkable, so the answer was Yes.

Then it was on to the design office where I learnt the skills of component design and design layouts. The biggest job of all was to take the detailed drawings of components and reassemble them to scale on a large drawing board to make sure everything would fit together. When the drawings were complete they were traced on linen for durability by young ladies known as tracers. A great opportunity to chat up the girls. I was rather shy, the girls were not!

During my time in the engine design drawing office I worked on the LR1, a long range jet engine with the by-pass principle. This is the concept used by modern jet engines today. This project was eventually cancelled when Power Jets became nationalised – an illustration of the incompetence which can arise when industries are nationalised.

When I was in the design office I was sent to a London exhibition to explain the workings of one of the cut away aircraft jet engines we had prepared at Lutterworth. It was a daunting prospect. In London, on my own, long days and numerous specialists asking very awkward questions, but very good experience at 19 years old. I stopped at an excellent hotel on Russell Square on company expenses. My first experience of luxury living.

While away one of my pals, Pete Rushall, had taken a girl to the Plaza cinema in Rugby. In between films there would always be a news film, who should be on the film but me, demonstrating the jet engine – Pete leapt in to the air shouting "that's Bill" much to the embarrassment of the young lady.

Next came the office where the component parts were developed and tested: fuel pumps, oil pumps, vacuum pumps, structures and other accessories. I now wore a sports coat and carried a six inch slide rule in my top pocket. By 1949 I was an engineer aged nineteen, albeit a very junior one, working under a senior engineer, still with Power Jets. My course at Leicester Technical College was of a very high standard and would finally lead to becoming a Chartered Engineer.

There was a lot to learn – thermodynamics, aerodynamics, hydraulics, reports to write and problems to solve. One challenge was to find a way of pumping bunker sea fuel oil if gas turbines were fitted to motor torpedo boats, a marine application.

When I was twenty I moved to the technical office of compressor tests. Power Jets had a test facility for gas turbine compressors which were driven by a destroyer marine steam turbine, the best way of generating the massive power required to test compressors. Not only did the facility test Power Jet designs but also tested and analysed compressors for other aero engine companies, including Armstrong Sidley, Rolls Royce and De Havilland. When not analysing test results I worked on the design of test systems including automatic shut down if compressors started to fail, special gear boxes and control systems.

During this time I finished my apprenticeship and had successfully completed my studies at Leicester.

Above: after five years of study only five out of thirty odd had obtained the qualifications required to eventually become chartered engineers. Myself in the centre.

CHAPTER 4

The Austin Motor Company

1951 – 1953

At this point the socialist government and the Prime Minister Attlee decided that nationalisation would be advantageous for Britain. Power Jets became the National Gas Turbine establishment, projects like the LR1, the first long range by-pass engine, was cancelled. I had to go to go to London for an interview where a group of civil servants, mainly from Woolich Arsenal interviewed me. They may have had a good knowledge of artillery but clearly did not know much about the aero engine business. I was offered a job as an Assistant Experimental Officer. I tolerated the job for a time but the air of despondency at Power Jets was such that I looked for another position. Many of the senior engineers were leaving, going to private companies and the USA.

Several senior men from Power Jets had moved to the English Electric at Rugby which had a project for a marine gas turbine frigate. I applied for a job there too and was offered a post in development. Although Rugby was my home town the move proved to be disastrous. The company was dreadfully old fashioned and my work was mainly structural testing. I felt my creative ability was being stifled and decided to look around.
After a few months I met an old friend at the pub and

when he arrived he was carrying a copy of the Coventry Evening Telegraph under his arm. On scanning the jobs column I saw a box number advertisement for a gas turbine engineer. I kept the paper and sent off my CV thinking it would be a post in Coventry. To my surprise I had a reply by return post from the Austin Motor Company asking me to attend an interview at Longbridge, Birmingham.

I put on my best suit, took the train to Birmingham, allowing plenty of time. On arrival at Birmingham I found I had to take a tram to Longbridge and it would take an hour. I was going to be late. When I arrived at the Austin Motor Company there was a tropical thunderstorm . Eventually I arrived at the office of Dr weaving, head of Research and Development. I stood before him dishevelled, in a pool of water, and the best part of an hour late. Despite my appearance he said sit down and we had a constructive discussion. I had an offer the following day which I could not refuse, as a research and development engineer with an excellent salary.

What a difference. Len Lord, the Managing Director for the Austin motor company had allocated half a million pounds per annum for R & D – probably ten million in today's money. Before getting involved in an advanced project I was told I had to familiarise myself with motor cars. All my experience was with jet aero engines. I was put to work with a senior engineer who had considerable experience of the design of vehicle petrol engines.

Tests were showing that on the test bed the engine destined for the new Austin Seven, later the Morris Minor and eventually the Mini, were all satisfactory. The figures from the tests which I was able to analyse accurately showed that the fuel consumption was satisfactory on the test bed. However a major problem on the cars which were being tested twenty four hours a day in eight hour shifts on a fixed circuit around the UK showed that the fuel consumption was unsatisfactory.

I was baffled, as was everyone else involved. Fortunately I went to the engine test beds to collect some more results when the tester was just shutting the engine down. Luckily I glanced at the fuel gauges and I saw one change rapidly showing a high fuel flow. I asked the tester to repeat the sequence and the result was the same. Once you can identify the problem it can generally be solved – there was a small spring loaded piston in the carburettor to give an additional jet of fuel when you opened the throttle to give acceleration. It was obvious the spring was going in to resonance at a certain engine speed and continuously pumping excessive fuel. I quickly redesigned the spring and engine tests showed the problem cured. It was then fitted to road test cars.

Although nobody congratulated me the "new boy" with no piston engine experience, was, perhaps, not bad after all. Many of the engineers in R&D were Austin trained graduates and some had doctorates of engineering. This bit of luck helped me earn their respect and they even fixed it for me to go to a free beer party that Len Lord gave to the Austin trained apprentices.

After about six months in development of conventional type engines I came in to my office and found to my surprise that my desk and contents had gone. I was told that I had been transferred to the Austin East Works which was almost a mile away. I duly reported there where the old aero engine test block had been transformed in to an absolutely splendid R&D facility - new desk, two telephones, cork floors, curtains in the office. Workshops, test facilities, wind tunnels, engine test bays, fitted shops et cetera, it was an R&D engineer's dream.

I had been recruited to work on a gas turbine car. After a short time we concluded that the project was not viable. This was to prove the right decision, although a competitor - the Rover company – continued with R&D on gas turbines instead of piston engines.

Amongst the projects I became involved in were two stroke engines, diesel engines for cars, and petrol injection. Alex Issigonis was working on the Mini at this time and we decided it was best to fit it with an established engine. I had a few conversations with Alex Issigonis and found him eccentric, full of ideas, and working himself on the drawing board. His design of the Mini was advanced and proved to be one of the most successful cars ever.

Len Lord was MD of the Austin Motor Company which employed several thousand people. He had an interesting policy of taking an hour off every day away from the main office block – known as the Kremlin. He would wander round any department and talk to anyone working there without informing the head of the department. He wore an old raincoat and was a small unimposing man. Of course panic would precede him and the word was "Len's on his way." One day he came to my desk, sat down and asked what I was doing. I explained I was investigating the problems of diesel engines in cars and the mechanics had just fitted a Perkins diesel engine in to an Austin car. He then said, "Outside my office midday next week, I want a ride!" Apprehensively I took the car as requested and drove it around the internal site roads, he just said, "Bloody noisy isn't it." And he disappeared in to the Kremlin. Len Lord was reported to have come across a gang of maintenance workers on a roof playing cards, he sacked them on the spot then sacked the charge hand and foreman, there were no tribunals in those days.

When I reached a lifetime ambition of being a chief engineer I would always take time off to walk around the office and talk to the design engineers, draftsmen, testers and people in the workshops. Although there were mixed views from the team, from "he's always on your back" to "it's good he takes an interest in what you are doing and makes constructive suggestions".

Although using a sharp pencil and a slide rule (later a calculator and computer) most of the time I had one interesting experience where my previous training proved advantageous. On test one of our experimental engines had broken a rocker (part of the valve gear) . A replacement forging would take three weeks, so I asked the fitter to make one from a solid piece of metal. "Can't be done," he said. I borrowed some tools from another fitter and proceeded to make the part myself. I had almost completed the item when there was a tap on my shoulder, it was the head of R&D Dr Weaving – "Very good Bailey, but we employ you to use your brains and not your hands". I didn't care the engine was back on test that afternoon and I had proved a point.

CHAPTER 5

Alvis

1953 to 1963

After two and a half splendid and happy years with the Austin research department I decided to move. I had met Joan, my wife to be, and Coventry was still a centre of the motor and aircraft industry. If I worked in Coventry I could live at home, see my fiancé more often, and extend my experience. There was a strong possibility that I Would be paid more. I wrote to Jaguar, Standard Triumph and Alvis with my CV and they all offered me an interview. I decided to go for an interview with Alvis being a relatively small but distinguished company.

My interview with the chief engineer of the aero division was very successful. I had the feeling that I knew more about centrifugal compressors, in this case for super charging, than he did. I asked for £18 a week but he said he could only offer me £16 a week. I agreed but said I would be looking for another position after 6 months at £18 a week, unless I had an increase to that amount. I went to see him after 6 months and he said he had already put the increase through.

To put things in perspective a thousand pounds per annum (£20 a week) would be an excellent salary. I was later to buy a half acre building plot at Berkswell for £600 and build a house for £3000.

My first challenge was to find out why some aero engines were being rejected on test beds for variations oil pressure. There was a rig test for pumps in the main assembly shop and when I asked the tester what the chirping noise was and he said sparrows in the roof I asked him why they stopped when they switched the test rig off. My experience at Power Jets with pumping systems was that inlet conditions were critical and the chirping sound was coming from a tiny air leak at the pump inlet. When we sealed the pump inlet with a special sealant the problem was solved. A small simple problem easily solved but it helped my initial credibility amongst the people who had been there many years and viewed new comers with some scepticism. In fact the head of all engine tests had actually complained to the chief engineer that I was rather a know-all, but after 3 months he changed his opinion, reporting that I was "bloody good". We were to work together very successfully for many years.

The position I accepted was development engineer. There was already another engineer working in this area and our work was basically to improve the reliability and performance of the radial air cooled engines. Any problems that the service department could not solve also came our way. Some of the problems we encountered were due to poor initial design and the main design and drawing office were not very pleased about myself and my colleague criticising and redesigning.

I was now 26 and had some very useful experience from

my previous work which I was able to put to good use. Whilst the test and build superintendent had considerable and invaluable experience and ability they were not trained in aero dynamics, structural design and thermal dynamics. The grape vine told me both the superintendents of the fitting shop and engine test thought I was insane to prevent fatigue failure of a part by making another part weaker. For the technically minded, weakening the connecting rods prevented the gudgeon pins failing while ensuring the connecting rods were still totally reliable.

Luck seemed to follow me in my engineering career. Alvis made engines for many different fixed wing aircraft and helicopters. One application was for a single engine short take off and land (stol) fixed wing aircraft, made by Scottish Aviation and called the Single Pioneer.

The UK was involved at that time in troubles in Aden on the Red Sea and the Single Pioneer was used for survey and other work. The problem was in that environment the engine would be running smoothly then violently shake as if there was an engine failure, then return again to smooth running. The pilots were dismayed by this phenomena and frightening experience. Engines were returned to Coventry and found on the test beds to be perfectly satisfactory. In an effort to do something I asked for an interview with a pilot and in due course several pilots arrived in Coventry and I had to do something! When I opened the door of the conference room there were several pilots and in the middle of the table was a small brass plate attached to a leather thong.

The plate was covered in Arabic. After introductions a pilot asked me what I thought the plate was for. Of course I hadn't a clue. Well said the pilot, when we go on a mission we wear one of these around our neck. If we crash or have a forced landing and the tribesmen appear we give them the brass plate. The plate offers a very substantial reward for the return of the pilot.

There are, said the pilot, two problems, the first being the tribesmen can't read, the second being that human testicles are much prized by the tribesmen's wives as fertility tokens and worn in a small bag around their necks. I flinched, was impressed, and after further discussion went away determined to solve the problem but not knowing where to start.

My best guess at that time was that it was a combustion problem related to ignition. By chance I was walking through the main assembly shop to my office when I saw an engine being unpacked from a crate that appeared to be very dusty. I guess the engine had been in storage for a long time but something prompted me to take a closer look and to my surprise found it was an engine returned from Aden. All engines coming from Aden are covered in dust, said the labourer unpacking the crate. A clue at last! I folded some dust in to a piece of paper and hurried to the metallurgy lab where we examined the dust under microscopes and determined the melting point of the dust. Silica! Said the metallurgist. The lab did more work on the dust and we had samples sent from Aden and reproduced the problem by injecting dust into an engine on test. Now we knew the problem was one of pre-ignition, created by the glowing silica and we could solve it: sweep the runways, water the runways, improve filtration and avoid dust storms where possible.

We could also reassure the pilots that the elevated temperatures caused by pre-ignition would melt the silica and clear the combustion chamber - a very undesirable situation but not as dangerous as it had appeared.

It was around 1960 and I arrived at my office and to my surprise the chief engineer was sitting in my chair. He seemed somewhat elated and explained there was a possibility of a substantial order. It was for around 400 engines if we could meet performance requirements. The engines were needed for a short take off and land (STOL) aircraft made by a Scottish company.

This potential order was from the Indian government to deal with the threat of a Chinese invasion. We were already supplying engines for the aircraft but not to the specifications now required. The special requirement was to permit the aircraft to land and take off on short air strips at high altitudes in the Himalayas where they feared the Chinese invasion would occur.

My secretary was immediately sent to Coventry to purchase an atlas so we could find out a little more about the Himalayas. We didn't know at the time exactly where the Himalayas were or what ambient conditions we were likely to encounter.
We quickly studied turbo charging, two speed super

charges and super charger redesign, but concluded for simplicity and reliability the best solution would be to sacrifice sea level performance to achieve high altitude requirement. Our proposal was accepted by both the Scottish company and the Indian government. We speedily modified control systems on two engines. Engine tests proved the engines to be satisfactory and flight testing confirmed the performance.

A team consisting of pilots, airframe fitters from Scottish aviation and one service mechanic from Alvis took the plane to India where a telegram confirmed that the Indian government were very pleased with the aircraft's performance. However they wanted trials on high altitude strips in the Himalayas before confirming the large order.

Twin Pioneer

Then there was silence. We eventually received a telegram from our man saying the aircraft had crashed killing everybody on board. It had been successfully demonstrated by the Scottish pilot. It was thought that the Indian pilot who had taken over that day had stalled the aircraft. Our service mechanic had not flown that fatal day and was the only survivor of the party. It was very much a matter of luck for him because the aircraft had sufficient payload without him on board. He had to bury the dead because the locals would not do so and he had walked out taking many days. Tensions between India and China had eased and there was no order. The end of a sad story, at least I thought it was.

Over twenty five years later in 1985 my life had changed considerably. My wife had died of cancer 2 years previously, my children were grown up and I was chief engineer of Massey Ferguson machinery division. I was browsing in the paper shop and picked up a climbing magazine and read an article on trekking in the Himalayas. I was intrigued and decided to go myself. I was hooked and the following year saw me on a tougher trek to the Kalapata mountain which looked down on Everest base camp.

We flew in to a small, then remote, airstrip at 10,000 feet known as Luckla. Here the aircraft had to land up hill and take off over a precipice. The airport office looked like a small hen house. After a tough but exhilarating trek in fantastic mountains our small party returned to the airstrip only to find that low cloud was preventing flying. Every day we would pack up our tents and kit and listen hopefully for an aircraft only to re-erect our tents and repeat the exercise the following day.

The Runway at Luckla in the Himalayas

In the group was a rugged Scottish farmer who had mountaineered extensively in Scotland. He was very enthusiastic about air craft and was always keen to get me to talk about aero engine development, helicopters etc. I was in my tent half asleep when my friend said he had found an aero engine and would I come and look at it. I emphatically said no, it would be a Pratt and Whitney engine that had been swapped and was not worth returning to Kathmandu. The aircraft that were used to fly to Luckla were "Otters" and used Pratt and Whitney engines. He was very persistent and I reluctantly dragged myself out of the sleeping bag to be shown to my amazement the specialised engine we had developed 25 years previously. I removed the identification plate and on my return checked with an old colleague it was indeed a very special engine. Was this just a remarkable coincidence or an uncanny twist of fate?

The remains of the specialised high altitude engine

A problem which came our way was that production

engines would occasionally seize and score the pistons. This was known as scuffing. It was only a problem when running an engine in, never a problem in service. While we experimented with different bore finishes etc we would think we had solved the problem and then it would re-occur. The reasons for this were not immediately apparent but by checking the records we were able to establish that the failures occurred at three week intervals. What did we do on production every three weeks? We eventually traced the problem to when fresh oil was put in the tanks on production test houses. Again once we knew the problem we were able to cure it by simply replacing 50% rather than all the oil at one time. It was evident that the used oil facilitated the running in process, possibly because of the carbon content.

Years later I was surprised to receive a phone call from one of my Alvis team who was then working for an aero engine company in the USA . He said they were having trouble with piston seizure on the aircraft used for water bombing forest fires. He told his boss that he didn't know the answer but he thought that I would be able to help. His boss said don't have any more phone conversations, get on a 'plane and go and see him! When he turned up I suggested a fairly simple remedy, remove the piston oil control ring and change the oil filters more frequently. After taking myself and my wife out to an expensive dinner he returned to the US and phoned me a couple of weeks later to say this had solved the problem.

After two years with Alvis my colleague Harry Cox left

the company to become engineering director of another firm. I became chief development engineer with a technical staff of about 10 including my secretary. Also in the team were 2 girls who did the more mundane work of routine calculations, drawing graphs etc which were presented to the engineers for analysis. They also worked a mechanical calculating machine similar to a type writer which made almost as much noise as a cement mixer. I had difficulty in persuading management to allow me to purchase the machine, which cost around £400 – a years salary for one of the girls who did the calculations.

One of these girls decided to leave the company and so we had a vacancy. I asked the personnel manager to find me a replacement . Very soon I had a call from him saying that he had just the girl for me and she was in his office and would I like to come up to see if she was suitable. I turned up in his office to see an exceptionally attractive, elegant young lady sitting beside his desk. I asked her several questions but thought it would be sensible to gracefully turn her down because I had an office full of young men between 20 and 30. However whatever questions I asked I could not fault her. She had a higher school certificate in mathematics, her printing was excellent, she was very intelligent and just what we needed. I asked her what she had been doing previously and she said modelling – when I asked her why she wanted to give up modelling she replied that she was sick of taking clothes off and on!

A dilemma - it would be unfair to turn her down and I offered her the job which she accepted. I was going on holiday and therefore I told my second in command to look after her. I told him about the "problem" of her attractiveness. He said ok but when he told the rest of the team they thought it was a wind up and the new female recruit would be extremely unattractive! It all worked out very well and my fears that they would be distracted were unfounded. From time to time the publicity director would ask if he could borrow "my" young lady. With her agreement he would get her to drape herself over the bonnet of a Grey Lady car, still made by Alvis, for advertisements, and reward her with flowers and chocolates. Grey Lady cars were, at the time, almost as prestigious as Rolls Royce.

Petrol Injection on the Grey Lady

Because of our team's considerable experience on fuel systems including petrol injection we were asked by the managing director whether we could fit a petrol injection system to the Grey Lady. We jumped at the opportunity and were given engines, car division labour and car test facilities. We successfully designed a system which pushed up the performance of the engine. After successful engine tests we fitted a modified engine to a car for road tests. At that time a long stretch of road was being built to bypass Meriden village. It was finished but not yet open to public traffic. When we approached the site manager he was very enthusiastic and said he would clear the road for us. We did a road test and did a maximum speed of 148 miles-per-hour – probably slightly downhill with a following wind! I was about to leave Alvis at this time and although I handed the project to another engineer the project died along with the Grey Lady which was the last Alvis car and the end of an era.

Another area of our aero engine work involved the Queen's Flight helicopter. The problems of reliability, pushing up performance and extending the life of engines were added to by a special request from the Queen's Flight. The Alvis chief engineer explained that the Queen's Flight, consisting of an aerodrome and numerous aircraft and staff, based at Benson, Oxfordshire, would be operating an S55 helicopter. The Queen would possibly fly in it, the Duke of Edinburgh and other members of the Royal family would definitely use it. The Duke had said he would like to fly it himself under the instruction of the Westland Chief pilot.

The question put to us was what else could we do to ensure maximum reliability. The Alvis engine already had two magnetos and sparking plugs per cylinder, so failure of one would only result in slight loss of power. The fuel systems were more of a hazard. I proposed that we could over ride the fuel control system in the event of failure, and that a pilot would be able to land the aircraft safely using a second system. The responsibility for the request fell on my department and our developments worked smoothly.

All went well and we considered the job completed, but the next I heard was that Royalty were going to fly and would I go to Benson and ensure everything was OK. This was really a job for our service department but they wanted me. The station commander invited me to lunch with him. Off I went, did a few checks aided by mechanics with beautifully polished tools and immaculate overalls. The helicopter was luxuriously upholstered so much so it was hard to find the cockpit! The lunch was excellent, served by a very pretty WAF and then I realised I was what the Americans called "the fall guy"; if the helicopter crashed for any reason it would be me in the witness box and possibly later in the Tower of London!

S 55 and the Queen's Flight

When I returned to Coventry I made it very clear that I would not go to Benson every time that Royalty flew and at least the blame for failure would be between service department and others. Subsequently the Fleet Air Arm who operated S55 helicopters heard about the safety system and said if it was good enough for the Queen it's good enough for us and all engines had the over ride system fitted.

Fleet Air Arm pilots came to Coventry to try out the device and I was horrified to see them cutting engines and restarting them in flight. I do not think they listened to my talk on how the system worked but had remarkable instincts. We never had a fuel system failure as far as I know, or lost a helicopter for this reason.

My English teacher at school had made a statement that had stayed in my mind "You will gain a great more if you save a man from drowning, than if you teach a man to swim". This was proved right to me on one of the Alvis assignments. Amongst the many applications we had for Alvis aero engines was the supply of engines for the RAF Provost training aircraft. We had reports that the engines were becoming unstable at certain altitudes and power with frightening effects. The result was that all Provost RAF aircraft were grounded until we were able to identify the cause of the problem. The civil aviation authorities were made aware of the problem and they also grounded all aircraft with this Alvis engine. The costs both in money are reputation to Alvis were enormous.

I had never met the managing director but he suddenly appeared in the main development office and then steamed in to my office demanding what we were doing about the problem. I tried to explain what I thought the instability problem was about but we needed to do many super charger and engine tests and analyse the results. I had put the whole technical team on to analysing results from engines tests together with aero dynamics analysis of the super charger. He was somewhat bewildered by the technical aspects of the work, much of which could not be explained in layman's terms, but said he would visit us again tomorrow and said I was to give the work priority.

When he turned up the following day he called me "Bill" and a I could report that we were making progress. However the next evening when he called he was shocked to find I had sent everybody home. The team had worked so hard so long that mistakes were being made in analysis and in my opinion it was far better to stop and start again fresh the following day. After 4 days of intensive work we were able to say positively that the problem was one of mismatching of engine and supercharger at certain conditions of altitude, speed and power. If you avoided these conditions it would be safe to fly. The managing director had called at my office every day and he was delighted that we knew what the problem was.

Now we had to find a way of re-matching the super charger to the engine. The obvious answer would be to remove the super charger which was an integral part of the engine to reduce its' capacity – a very expensive and time consuming exercise.
Having slept on the problem I had an idea. Why not leak some of the air delivered by the super charger back in to the engine in-take. My initial thoughts were to design a valve for this purpose but further thinking and calculation showed that by drilling two small holes in the in-take and leaking back air we could in effect reduce the capacity of the super charger. This modification could be carried out without even removing the engine from the aircraft. It was a spectacular success.

A few days later I was called to the chief engineers office where he said the MD had instructed him to give me a twenty per cent increase in salary. I then negotiated a ten per cent increase in salary for the rest of the team. It was certainly more profitable "to save the man from drowning than to teach him to swim"!
One of the problems we faced with engines in the

helicopter application was restarting and slow running at high altitudes. At altitudes of around 14,000 feet the density of the air is less than half that at sea level and the temperature is as low as -15 degrees centigrade. Both starting and slow run were virtually impossible in these conditions and we were working on a two stage injection nozzle to overcome this difficulty. I had a phone call from the chief engineer who said that Westlands had requested that I should meet them at Yeovil to discuss the problem. On arrival I was handed a parachute by the chief test pilot, Slim Sear, who said come on I'll show you the problem. I immediately said that I knew what the problem was and that I thought we had a solution. Never mind, he said, while you are here let me show you. I was very nervous to say the least when he flew to around 12,000 feet and cut the engine and then tried to restart. It was around 10,000 feet before he was able to restart. In retrospect I think it was a ploy to get us to work faster.

Back in Coventry we were progressing well with the two stage nozzle. It was going to solve the problem of being able to land and take off on mountains of possibly 15000 feet. It meant that very small quantities of fuel would be needed finely atomised for the slow run conditions; but very large quantities of fuel would be required for maximum power at take-off.

The small atomising nozzle within the main nozzle which we developed was working well on flow tests and engine tests and all that was required was flight testing. The phone rang – it was Slim Sear, the somewhat maverick chief test pilot from Westland helicopters. He asked me how the problem of slow run was progressing.

I explained that we were confident that we had solved the problem but flight testing would be necessary. How long would it take to fit the replacement nozzle, he asked. I said, About an hour. He said, Clear the cricket pitch I'm on my way – and put the phone down. We quickly arranged for fitters to be available, informed Alvis security, and the helicopter was with us and the nozzle fitted within a couple of hours.

Small boys came from everywhere with their noses pressed against the wire. Helicopters were not common then. The pilot took off and returned within an hour, landed, gave me the thumbs up sign and shouted he was on his way to Austria to demonstrate. We subsequently got the order.

When I got back to my office I was told that the chief engineer wished to see me urgently. He told me I was never to do anything like that again. The police, the aviation authorities and the council had all complained to the MD – you were supposed to get permission to land helicopters on cricket pitches!

We were fitting engines to a wide range of fixed wing and helicopter aircraft. For engine performance analysis it was necessary to be able to correct to a standard the performance which was affected by temperature, barometric pressure, altitude and humidity. To this end we varied test bed conditions artificially and were able to standardise and predict performance. We were able to get down to temperatures as low as minus thirty degrees centigrade by pumping a mixture of methanol and solid carbon dioxide through a number of car radiators. The solid carbon dioxide was supplied by courtesy of Wall's Ice cream.

The adverse effects of humidity had been identified as very important when helicopters were used in the Burmese jungle to evacuate the wounded soldiers.
I was summoned and told that I was to go to the Admiralty together with the Westland chief engineer, once a week, to report on helicopter developments. I was not sure what it was about but I went off to the |Admiralty in London. Most of the people went to the meeting wearing bowler hats and the meeting was chaired by an admiral wearing lots of gold braid.

Because a significant part of the power of the engine is used to lift the helicopter the payload is significantly affected by ambient conditions. However I pointed out that it was possible to predict the acceptable payload by analysis of the ambient conditions.

"Right," said the Admiral, the man with all the gold braid. I want you with us. I did not know where they were going but it sounded dangerous so I quickly said, calling him sir, that I would have coloured charts et cetera by the end of the week to enable his officers to predict the performance and payload. He reluctantly grunted approval and I was later to find out that the outing was for the invasion of Suez. I think this was the first time helicopters were used from aircraft carriers for military purposes.

Virtually all the problems we experienced we were able

to solve and rectify. However there was one outstanding problem we never did solve. This was the time of the Cold War and helicopters were used to listen for and locate Russian submarines. The role was known as "dunking", an expression used when one dips a biscuit in tea – in this case very sophisticated electronics were lowered in to the sea from a helicopter to locate the nuclear submarines of the Russians. It was said that the sophisticated electronics were as valuable as the helicopter.

The helicopters had to hover very close to the sea. Several helicopters with everyone on board did not return from these missions and we never found out why. Was it due to engine cutting for an instant? Or the ingress of salt spray? Was it a rogue wave? Was it enemy action? Was it seaweed or debris snatching at the device? The device could be disengaged so whatever it was must have happened pretty quickly. It was only when they were dunking that they were in danger. It remained for me the one unsolved problem despite extensive research.

Another project that was given to me while I was at Alvis led to the development of a drone engine. At the end of the war unmanned aircraft and rockets, V1's and V2's had proved a great threat to the Allies. If Hitler had waited a little longer for his scientists and engineers to develop the V1 and V2 rockets England would have had no alternative but to capitulate. To be fair, the Allies did get there first with the nuclear bomb.

Around 1962 we were asked at Alvis by the Government

whether we could develop a small engine of less than 100 horse power suitable for target and drone work. The engine to be of high performance, low cost, and low fuel consumption such that the range was substantial and could possibly return to base with data to be used again. After studying the problem I concluded that a multi cylinder piston engine running at high speed would offer the best solution. However such an engine would present inherent crank shaft problems and require a propeller reduction gear. I therefore proposed a unique design using a cam instead of a crank shaft. A reduction gear would not be required and we decided we should, with government approval, build an experimental research engine. The engine by virtue of a two lobe cam would have a sequential firing order giving an induction ram effect, an aspect that was never investigated.

Other aspects of the design were that the piston action was simple harmonic where as normal piston engines have a modified simple harmonic action by virtue of connecting rods. The simple harmonic action was chosen because of ease of manufacture for the prototype cam. It was possible that the cam design could be made such that the induction stroke was slower than the expansion stroke, thus improving breathing and performance. Because of the unique concepts there were many aspects of the proposal needing investigation but there was no doubt that the design was remarkably simple and very suitable for an expendable engine such as drones, targets et cetera.

Front view of the small prototype engine.

The dismantled prototype engine.

I was given a limited budget for the project and we designed and built a cam engine for research purposes. Preliminary testing, including a 50 hour endurance test, showed the concept had great potential but that like all projects further work was required. I was then informed that the government had stopped the project and I was to stop all work on the engine. Both myself and my department were disgusted. After all the work we had put in even a limited budget would have allowed us to confirm the project. Neither Alvis nor the Government understood the potential of this engine. Alvis did not have an engineering director on the board to fight our case and I realised that I was, sadly, working for the wrong company as the aero engine division was going nowhere.

Time to look around! I should point out that the shop floor, tool room and test departments were second to none and I would be sad to go. Also I had a team around me that I would be reluctant to leave. They were good days and I had been doing for a living what many people would have loved to have done for a hobby. However at thirty seven years old it was now or never.

Eventually this Alvis factory in Coventry, which was employing over 2000 workers, disappeared to be replaced by supermarkets and MacDonald's. Although no longer working for Alvis I could not drive past the site without some anger as I mourned the loss of so much UK engineering which at one time led the world.

Post war Alvis front office block – the original factory having been destroyed by bombing. This site now a shopping centre.

CHAPTER 6

Massey Ferguson

1963-1988

Having made up my mind to leave Alvis I decided to explore other possibilities. Although there were obvious other motor companies, Jaguar, Rover, British Motor Company and others the grape vine said that Massey Ferguson was seeking engineers and had opened a new research and development centre. It was also said that Massey Ferguson paid 25% more than elsewhere for the same situation.

Engineering was led by Dr Willets, a qualified engineer, and he was on the Board of Directors. Dr Willets had a reputation for making sure that engineering was well represented and that his engineers had status.

I went for an interview which went well but I was disappointed to be offered a job on farm machinery rather than on tractors. I understood that the tractor division also wanted me but the chief engineer of farm machinery insisted that he interviewed me first. The offer was for a project engineer leading a small team of 5 draughtsmen, a section leader and a junior engineer – no secretary. It was a real loss in status but a better salary. I was angry with Alvis and took the job.
I had said at the interview what if I have difficulty with handling this new type of engineering? They simply said

if you are good at the job you will progress, if not we will lose you.

My first task was to sort out linkage problems between tractors and machinery; the machinery had been getting bigger and the current draw bars were breaking. My new design, backed up by calculation and rig and field testing, was successful. One significant development was a redesign of the swinging draw bar where I increased the section transversely thus making it stronger and more resilient. I also developed a forged end which allowed me to get adequate strength. One important aspect was that the new draw bar was directly interchangeable with the draw bars which were failing so it was an instant success.

I insisted that every component was calculated, tested, and the results recorded. The calculations and results were filed for reference and available to the team. The discipline of recording and storing calculations and test results in a manner that made them readily accessible had been developed by me at Alvis. These disciplines were new to Massey Ferguson but quickly proved to be advantageous.

More work came my way and I was given a major project to work with ICI (Imperial Chemical Industries) to sow seeds in to ground that was not tilled. It was thought that this would be a revolution in farming. We built a successful experimental direct drilling machine but I had my doubts about the techniques other than for specialised applications. MF agreed with my views and I was then asked to take over all planting machinery. The senior experienced engineer who was responsible for planting machinery would be working for me. To my surprise he came to me, shook hands and said he was very happy to work for me.

An experimental drilling machine for conventionally prepared land had already been built but early tests showed that it was unsatisfactory. It had been explained early on in the new project that marketing would get together a specification based upon market research with farmers and we would design a machine to meet their requirements. I studied the marketing specification and spent a day doing basic design calculations. Performance on inclines, different soil types, tyre types and machine geometry. I then asked for a meeting with marketing. We all assembled in a conference room. I said I had done some basic calculations for their proposal. They smiled. Then I said there is only one problem. They smiled again. "We don't make a tractor big enough to pull it." They stopped smiling….

Although I always listened to marketing and enjoyed good relations with sales, marketing and farmers, I would not let their views dominate my design. Their views were often influenced by customers and farmers thus preventing advanced thinking and innovation. One of my favourite sayings was "what if you asked your grandfather what he would like best of all for entertainment on a Sunday night. He might say, for example, a new violin. What if we gave him a box in a corner of a room with coloured pictures of what is currently happening in the USA? The reply would be, don't be daft."

The same applied to asking a pilot what he required in a new aircraft. The answer would have been a more powerful engine and propeller. How about an aeroplane without a propeller? The reply would be the same, don't be daft. My policy was always to think of other ways to do things and not be constrained by convention.

An MF tractor pulling the smallest drill of the range. The small tyres were not popular and eventually all were fitted with larger tyres.

I now had a good team of draftsmen and design engineers working for me and we set about designing a new range of seed drills. I insisted on a disciplined approach with innovation and the machines were an instant success. The machines won many awards including the prestigious design award given by the Duke of Edinburgh – the only farm machine to win this design award. The previous years the design award winners were given a trip on Concord. The following year, when we won the award, we were taken round the new Birmingham Exhibition Centre, what a let down!

More work came my way and eventually I was promoted to chief engineer and I was in charge of all farm machinery other than tractors and combine harvesters. Because of my engine experience I was also asked to be responsible for tractor engine and tractor performance analysis. I was given extra staff to deal with this added responsibility.

The MF 30 Drill, one of the range of prize winning machines.

An interesting problem was when Ford tractors claimed that our tractors did not give the engine performance as published. They had one of our tractors in their test facility and were prepared to demonstrate this. This was part technical but also political and the problem was passed to me. I arranged to meet them at the Ford test facility at Dagenam and they were indeed able to show me that the performance was down. I looked at their instrumentation, method of calculation etc but could not fault it. Puzzled, I had an inspired thought and asked whether I could look outside the test facility.

They seemed surprised but agreed and when I went outside the building I found the air intake was close to the exhaust; I pointed out that this could be the problem. They quickly piped the intake away from the exhaust, problem solved! The performance was as MF had proclaimed. Apologies from Ford. I had been there less than an hour.

It was about this time I was again offered promotion in MF. This time it was for the post of technical Director on the industrial machinery side (earth moving equipment) in Manchester. But I preferred to remain chief engineer of the farm machinery, enjoying being close to engineering with a good team. By this time the farm machinery group had moved to Stoneleigh, a country park location, as a separate division from tractors. Our situation here was ideal. I could walk out the office door and watch machines on test in beautiful parkland.

Despite my commitments leading the farm machinery team I travelled frequently and found myself on special overseas missions. These were additional to the many visits made to North America and Europe.

One day the managing director of Europe came in to my office, put his hand on my shoulder and said, I want you to visit some of the "overseas territories"; by this he meant Middle Eastern countries, Africa and possibly areas behind the Iron Curtain. He felt marketing did not know enough about the various machines' potential for us to gain maximum sales by fulfilling their special requirements.

I said I didn't think I could leave the office for that length of time. He said, I'm not asking you, I'm telling you. So that was that. First of all I went to Saudi Arabia and other middle- eastern territories.
I was interested to see centre pivot irrigation where water is pumped from below the desert and they were able to grow two crops of wheat per year. Another smaller scale method of growing crops was to pump water from below the desert and then release it downhill making and breaking sequentially a series of soil and rock dams to irrigate the fields. This was ok but I immediately saw that there was room for substantial improvements by adapting a special front end loader. I made a sketch of what I proposed and what we could possibly provide. My Arab contact, asked for the sketch, kept it and eventually returned it to me. When I returned to the UK marketing said we have received an order from Saudi Arabia for 500 attachments "as Bill Bailey's sketch". What is it? And what do we charge for it? I quickly put a design engineer and two draughtsmen on the job and in a couple of days we had completed the drawings and costings. It was up to marketing what they were going to charge for it.

Whilst in Saudi Arabia I got on rather well with one of the wealthy Saudi dealers and he said he would come and visit me in the UK and we would go to France and I could take him around the various clubs – The Crazy Horse, Moulin Rouge etc. When I returned to the UK I told the MD of this proposal and said I would send a student to France for my friend if he turned up. The MD said if he wants to go, you go. Fortunately he never did turn up but I received a Christmas card from him for several years.

Discussing crops in Zambia

The following year I toured South Africa, Zambia, Kenya visiting dealers, engineering companies and farmers. Again the experience was invaluable and I was able to solve problems and make suggestions. One

instance was where we had bearing failures on a machine. When I saw it the operators were not lifting the machine out of work at the end of the field and with the aid of power steering were able to force the machine around the corner: the solution was simple – just instruct the operators how to work the machine.
While in Zambia I met an English farmer who found my views on the future farm machinery interesting and very kindly invited me to stay at his farm for the weekend. He intended to fly me over the Victoria Falls but was unable to get the requisite petrol.

However when he learnt of my interest in shooting he said there were plenty of Guinea fowl on his farm and he would provide me with a shot gun. There were however a few problems. First, there were leopards in the rock outcrops and it was just possible that one might drop on you; secondly, whatever you do don't shoot a baboon, or shoot close to them, otherwise the whole tribe will attack you and tear you to pieces. When I arrived at the farm two of his black workers were skinning a huge yellowish snake which he explained, although poisonous, were good eating. I politely declined the offer to go shooting!

I did however have one of the best meals of my life: local South African wine served with barbequed steak which had been reared "on the hoof" over large areas of marginal lands.

On returning to England I conceded that the MD had been right. I had solved problems and had gained considerable knowledge of conditions abroad which would enable Massey Ferguson to extend their overseas sales.

Another unusual trip was to Russia in the 1960's. The cold war was thawing and the Russians were anxious to improve their farm machinery and do some kind of technological deal. I had come alone to join a delegation of European agricultural engineer specialists.
When I arrived in Moscow after long and vigorous passport examinations I was taken to what was claimed to be the biggest hotel in the world. It was too late to eat but I was desperate for a beer. I had read that on each floor there would be a person called a "dinashoi" to help you with any problem. Off I went and found my "dinashoi" chatting to an army officer. After some difficulties in communication the Russian officer took me to a room full of very drunk officers most of whom were asleep on the floor. He poured me a huge vodka, I think he said "Dos devana", so I said "dos devana" and downed the vodka in one. He then poured me another and we repeated the process. I wondered when this was going to stop but he handed me a bottle of beer, I saluted him and he saluted me and I left the room.

There appeared to be no restaurants in Moscow and the food and lodging was pretty basic. Wine, beer and so called champagne were all served in the same type of bottle. The waitresses did not seem to bother whether they served you or not. One bright spot was when I left my overcoat at a hotel cloakroom an elderly lady snatched it away and when I returned all the buttons had been re-sewn. In an effort to provide everybody with a job there were some surprising services. I was in a splendid deep bath when I noticed a chain with a handle and being inquisitive I pulled it, to be surprised by a big Russian lady rushing in to see if I was drowning. Unknown to me it was an emergency system.

Speaking to Eastern Bloc representatives

One thing I did notice was the way the Russians respected their professional engineers. We arrived late one evening at a hotel restaurant to be told that it was full. When we said that we were engineers the man said "this way sirs" – so different to the UK!

It was a good trip. I was surprised how badly designed their farm machinery was but was careful to make suggestions rather than be too critical. We did not do a deal with Russia but we were able to help them in some areas and perhaps contributed to East–West relationships.

I also visited Poland several times. The Poles were anxious to update their farm machinery including tractors. Again they did not have money but prepared to supply components to our drawings in return for technology. On one particular trip I was accompanied by my equal, the chief engineer, from our North American operations.

When I met him at the airport in Warsaw he said, "Bill this is sure going to be hard work but we Americans are used to hard work," - the inference being that we in the UK were idle! As the trip progressed I noticed that he was weakening – was it due to double vodkas at 9am or the tough schedule of visiting farms, factories and universities? One evening after dinner he said "Bill I think I will have an early night, I'm about all in." I said I was going to have a couple of drinks in the bar. When there I was propositioned by an attractive prostitute. It should be remembered that a few American dollars were worth a fortune at that time. I explained I was not interested but suggested that if she try Room number - , giving her Bob's room number, my colleague would definitely be interested.

In the morning Bob emerged bleary eyed and I said "you look a bit jaded" – he said "Bloody women were knocking on my door all evening, I did not get to sleep until 1 in the morning. I said never mind you will feel better after you have had the couple of 8am vodkas at the next visit. He did not smile.

Despite extensive travels over the country we never did a deal. Unfortunately their operations were not of a standard that would enable us to do a deal. Despite being willing and enthusiastic their factories were not of an adequate standard for our machinery.

In the mid 1980's the managing director of Massey Ferguson and I were asked to attend a select committee in the House of Commons. This was to discuss the prospects of farm machinery business in the UK. I pointed out that smaller companies did not have rescources to design and develop sophisticated farm machinery. They also lacked the marketing network to sell machinery on a world wide basis. They were however excellent and efficient manufacturers. The formula we were using where MF designed and marketed, but small companies manufactured, was a proven one.

Although there was no conclusion at the meeting I was able to negotiate a government grant of half a million pounds for research and development of new machines. This was a considerable sum in those days.
We had just got the new organisation up and running when we were informed that we were to be sold off to a European consortium of farm machinery manufacturers. The staff were to be transferred to the tractor division. I was offered early retirement after having been with MF for 25 years. My contract said they were to give me a year's salary. I had no alternative but to accept. But no sooner had I accepted the deal than I was asked to stay on by MF to facilitate the change over. The purchsers were Greenland, a consortium of well known European machinery manufacturers. They agreed to pay me a

substantial salary for that year.

This worked well for me and the European company were very pleased with the work I did for them. Before the year was up they offered me a chief engineer's job in Holland and said I could fly home every weekend at their expense. I turned down their offer but agreed to work for them as a consultant. This would enable me to disappear for my high mountain expeditions for weeks at a time.

If I had had a penny for this small device I invented for Greenland I would have been a wealthy man!

During the time I worked for the Holland based group I developed several patentable designs. One very simple but patentable device permitted the easy removal of wearing parts from two days work to less than two hours was copied by a competitor. I was asked to advise the patent lawyer on what to say. It took me less than a morning's work to point out that my idea was novel. It had made the agricultural press. When I invoiced my employer for half a days work on the subject the MD rang me to say he had a complaint. I had not charged enough! The patent lawyer they had instructed was charging more per hour than I had charged per day.

I was then approached by other law firms to see if I would take on more expert witness work and was offered, by engineering standards, astronomical fees. I did several jobs of this kind before turning this work down because I could not guarantee being available in the UK. My overseas mountain expeditions took priority. A decision I did not regret.

Thus after fifty years my engineering career came to an end except for an occasional phone call. If I had my time over again I would do the same. A little sad at the decline of engineering in the UK, every company I worked for has now been replaced by housing estates, supermarkets and MacDonalds. At one time we led the world in many areas of engineering. Nevermind we don't need to actually design and make anything, we have the City!

PART THREE

LIFE

1945 -2015

CHAPTER 7

Boating, shooting, cycling……

Despite wishing to plan one's life, chance and luck play the most important role in determining what actually happens. After leaving school and pursuing an engineering career I had little time to spare on my hands. We did have an annual fortnights holiday. On leaving school two of my eighteen year old pals - they were a year or two older than me - said they were going to hire a sailing boat on the Norfolk Broads. Would I like to come? My mother said "you're not going". I said I had saved the requisite £9, which I had raised by breeding tame rabbits for their fur. She relented.

Off we went by train to Oulton Broad. We took a big trunk packed with some food, a few spare clothes and a book on sailing. On arrival a gentleman rowed us out to the boat and said, she's all yours, and rowed away. After a bit of experimenting we got underway and sailed around the Broad before going down the river.

On one exciting occasion when we needed to lower the mast to go under a low bridge the rigging became tangled. I had to climb the mast, there was a strong tide carrying us towards the bridge and I still remember the bridge looming larger by the second.

One slight mishap, we moored for the night by a pub where I continued my apprenticeship on sailing and drinking. I was woken in the night with things sliding around the floor. We did not realized the river was tidal and the tide had gone out and the boat was suspended by the mooring ropes.

On another occasion we anchored in the middle of a Broad and rowed to a pub. We had pulled the white awning over the well of the boat, which in effect extended the cabin for sleeping. On returning in the dark, in high spirits, we climbed aboard and a voice called that there was somebody in his bunk. There was a shout – "It's not our boat" ! A mad scramble then we rowed away.

Back to the Broads the following year for a week, after that we hired a boat on the Avon and Severn. We managed to get rather drunk on cider at Upton on Severn and were incapable of rowing against the tide to our boat moored on the opposite bank. We ended up tying the dingy up, crossing the bridge to our boat and going back next day for the dingy.

During my apprenticeship I had virtually no spare time. What time I did have was taken up with study. However some Saturday afternoons I would go rabbit shooting with my cousin on my Uncle's farm at Hillmorton. In addition to the farm they had a milk round and we were able to sell rabbits to customers at 2shillings and 6pence each. When we shared the proceeds it was often greater than my wages as an apprentice.

We had several ferrets, Gracie in particular, would follow you like a dog. Another pair we named Phillip and Elizabeth after royalty. One ferret however was useless and my cousin suggested we should half starve it and use it for ratting – there was a huge bank in the old orchard riddled with rat holes. Obviously we could not use the purse nets used for rabbiting, the rats would simply run through them. What we did use were tin cans, open at both ends, with ladies' old stockings tied over them. You simply pushed the stocking in to a hole and watched the stocking become alive as the rat came in to it such was the rat's fear of ferrets. We quickly picked the stocking up with the rat in it and banged it on the ground, which rapidly disposed of the rat.

The farm was mainly a dairy one and the milk was delivered by pony and trap to the customers. We had fixed hooks on the side of the trap and offered the rabbits for sale. The demand at the end of the war always exceeded the supply and my cousin eventually took orders to ensure the people at the end of the round had an opportunity to get a rabbit. We often stopped till dark in an effort to meet demand. I was often reprimanded by my cousin if I shot at but missed a rabbit, he would jokingly say, "hey, that one was ordered!"

A few miles from Hillmorton there was another farm with wooded banks that were riddled with rabbits. We went to see the farmer with a view to purchasing the rabbit rights for a year. He firmly dismissed the proposal and obviously thought we could not control the rabbit population. As we walked away somewhat despondently down the drive I had an idea. Why don't we offer him 1 shilling for every rabbit we get? It means he can have other people there if we are not effective. We returned, knocked on the door and apprehensively put the proposal to him. His wife looked over his shoulder and said oh that's very fair and the farmer agreed to the plan. Most Saturdays we would get more than 10 rabbits and hand over the 10 shillings plus to the delight of the farmer's wife .

My cousin who was a few years older than me told me of some of the amorous ladies on the milk round. I thought they were just tales and not to be believed. However on turning up one morning my uncle said Tony has the flu and could I take his place on the milk round. I agreed and was instructed to knock on the door and shout "Milko" and wait as some clients would wish to pay the bill. This I did and at one house was welcomed by a lady wearing a dressing gown and nothing else, completely unbuttoned down the front. Oh, she said, I thought it was Tony. We did look a little alike, just shows how wrong I had been about the famous milk round.

When I was offered the position with the Austin motor company I had to find myself accommodation in Birmingham. The land lady was the worst cook I ever met, but I was within walking distance of the Austin works which was very convenient. I had to put up with four of her atrocious dinners but would cycle the 29 miles back home on the Friday night and cycle back before breakfast on Monday. These were my cycle racing days so that added to my training program.

Whilst in digs I did not stay with the family one single

evening. You could select courses on all kinds of subjects at a further education college. I undertook a Spanish course in preparation for a proposed cycle adventure in Spain. Half way through the course the lecturer suggested I share a text book with a very attractive redhead. I never bought the book!

A work mate suggested we take another course, ball room dancing, which would, we hoped, introduce us to some young ladies. To our horror when we entered the room there was not another man in sight and we were grabbed by big middle aged ladies and whisked around the room. Exhausted at the end of the session we were making our escape when the male pianist said to us, "Are you coming to the pub?" We eagerly said yes and when we reached the pub he found a piano and sat down to play. He was exceptionally talented and the room quickly filled with people buying him beer until the top of the piano was laden with full glasses. He said drink up lads, see you next week. Another dilemma – we did attend the dancing lessons several times and enjoyed the free beer.

Ultimately my friend and I escaped from our digs and rented our own flat. It was upstairs and very small but we were able to cook our own food, what a relief.

Once a week we would go to the centre of Birmingham where we imposed on ourselves a challenge. We would have 4 half pints each, never go in the same pub again, and never pass a pub. We finished up in some strange places but had some interesting experiences.

During these years life was tough with work and intensive studying; therefore the annual holiday had special significance. I was a little surprised when one of my friends from schooldays turned up and said that he and two of his friends were planning to cycle north to Scotland through Derbyshire, Northumberland and back through the Lake District. They proposed to stop at youth hostels. They were looking for a fourth rider as they felt that would make the riding more sociable. I expressed some doubt about my cycling ability but I had been cycling to work fourteen miles return every day and enjoyed it. Pete said he would arrange a long ride before the holiday as training. This was a turning point in my life when I said OK.

Pete arranged a ride to Brighton and back, to visit my grandmothers. It was about 300 miles in four days. We stopped at youth hostels and although it was my first long distance cycle ride I had no problems.

When I turned eighteen I was able to have a pint of beer legally. In a Derbyshire pub early on in the trip we were asked to judge the local beauty competition because we would be unbiased. What a privilege! The four of us sat on the stage of the local hall while the local lovelies paraded in front of us.

We were permanently hungry because food, including bread, was rationed. We would buy a loaf everyday with our coupons and we had a pot of jam. This provided us with a midday treat. One day a dog came along and stole our loaf – with our only knife in it. We pursued it unsuccessfully. To stave off hunger we would stop off at farms and ask to buy a pint of milk to put in our bottles. Invariably our offer of cash was refused. The Scots were particularly generous and often gave us cake which defied the belief that Scots are parsimonious.

What emerged during the trip was that I was a natural cyclist. When asked to join the trip I had not known that the other three were members of the Rugby racing club and were competent racing cyclists. When we came to long steep climbs there would be a competition amongst us to see who was over the top first. I was nearly always first and still recall the pleasure, and pain the challenge gave me. Getting over the Kirkstone Pass in the Lake district was particularly elating.

My pals said there was no question about it, I should become a member of the Rugby racing club with them, and compete in the Novice twenty-five mile race. My time was a reasonable one hour seven minutes. It was a winning time and from then on the racing became a passion. I rapidly became involved both socially and competitively.

Winning the November handicap cyclo cross 1950

There were different types of cycling competitions available to us: time trialing (where you raced a set distance against the clock), cross country, grass track racing, hard track racing, and mass start. At that time mass start racing was not allowed on roads.

Having tried time trialing and deciding it was not for me, I entered the open cross country race called The November Handicap. This was a twelfth mile cross country, muddy track, grass and ploughed fields etc. To my surprise I finished 7th in a field of over 100 riders. My team mate Bernard Harris, a better road man than me, said "once you pick up your bike and run with it there is no way I can stay with you." Concluding that I could excel in this cyclo cross I trained the following year and finished 4th in the same event.

By then I decided that I could win the event and I should go flat out from the start so that I would not be slowed by other riders in my way. This I did and when I looked over my shoulder there was no one to be seen. Panicking a little, "had I gone off course?" Then I saw marshals in the distance. All was well. Looking over my shoulder frequently I did not see anybody and finished at the top of a long hill well ahead of the field. I was thirty seconds in front of my nearest rival and had achieved my ambition. My two team mates were not far behind and we had won the team prize

In the summer we would frequently ride on grass tracks. This was very popular, especially in mining towns and one could find an event which included cycling and running most weeks in the summer. Rugby had 3 meetings and I can still recall the pleasure chatting up the delightful female runners in their scanty kit. It was not uncommon to have over a thousand spectators and there was always an illegal book maker or two on the course. You could bet on yourself if you wished. I was never a cycle sprinter but enjoyed the five mile race.

Other interesting races were a "no-distance" race when the bell went when there was one lap to go. Sometimes it paid to make your bid early in the race and take a chance of being away when the bell went. Another race was "devil take the hindmost" where the last 2 riders were pulled out every lap with the last 3 riders competing at the end for 1st, 2nd and 3rd. There were always crashes and pile ups on these grass track races, to the joy of the spectators. Often riders would suffer a broken collar bone. One of our Rugby lads had his ear go through a chain ring with evenly spaced perforations! Generally one got away with bumps and bruises.

A big event which went back to Victorian times was where cross country cyclists competed against runners. Cyclists versus harriers at Walsall in the Black Country. I was going reasonably well and carrying my bike on my shoulder in a very rough patch when I caught a runner. I shouted, coming through! – the polite way of overtaking somebody. But the runner would not get out of my way. Eventually I saw my chance and overtook the runner, flipped my bike, and he was pushed off the narrow path. I forgot the matter completely but when I went in to the office the following Monday a colleague said: saw you on the telly (black and white, small screen in those days), pushing that poor runner off the path! I had my leg pulled for a week, being called "killer Bailey".

Mass start "road racing" was held in the summer on disused aerodromes, parks, or private circuits. Our

Rugby club, which initially had focused on time trials, developed a very successful mass start team of which I was a part.

During the 1950's a group from the Rugby Racing Club would take their annual holiday on a cycling trip of around fourteen days. Following the UK adventure which had introduced me to cycling and racing, the next trip was to southern Ireland.

Ireland was selected by our group of six because food was not rationed. We cycled from Rugby to Holyhead, stopping at Bangor to go to a local dance on the way. We arrived at Holyhead early in the morning and crossed to Dublin. We had breakfast in Dublin and it was unreal to have as much food as we wished after years of rationing. Sugar in our tea, two eggs and bacon, fried bread ….. one of our group was sick not being used to so much food.

Before departing for Ireland my older sister had asked me to get her some stockings, stockings then being virtually unobtainable in England. So while in Dublin I went in to a shop to purchase the stockings I was accompanied by one of my pals who said, what a good idea I'll get some too, for my girlfriend. I said, what size does she take? He said he didn't know. Jokingly I said, go and ask a girl in the street what size stocking she takes, thinking he would be told to mind his own business. Surprisingly he came back in to the shop smiling saying a very nice girl had been most helpful.

From Dublin we cycled across southern Ireland. A memorable event was on a Sunday. We arrived in the small Irish town of Kenmare. It had been the day of the National Drag Hunt where they drag a scented bag across the moors and race the hounds. We arrived after the event and there was not a sober person in the town. The man at the hotel reception desk was so drunk that I had to write the names in the register. We joined in the festivities and I recall standing on a table with the local policeman, I wore his policeman's hat:

"Goodbye, Goodbye, it's time I sought a foreign clime, Where I may find there are hearts more kind than I leave behind.
And so, I go, to fight the savage foe, Although, I know, that I'll be sometimes missed by the girls I've kissed......"

Next morning with hellish hangovers we set off again.
After spending time at Killarny on the west coast we went to Belfast in Northern Ireland to take the boat back to England In Belfast, near the Docks, one of our team went in to the local pub and asked where there was a good place to stay. He was directed to a small boarding house around the corner where we subsequently booked in. The breakfast and the rooms were good and the manager very friendly. But we established later that it was a brothel.

France was the next year's objective. We met in the Dirty Duck Pub in Rugby in the evening to cycle down overnight to Newhaven. We stopped in Hyde Park to make a cup of tea where we were questioned by two policemen. We got to Brighton in time for breakfast under the promenade then on to Newhaven in time to get the early morning ferry to Dieppe. Our goal was to get to the Mediterranean coast and back within our fortnight's holiday.

On arrival in France we met some French racing cyclists who suggested we came over the following year and rode in the annual road race around Dieppe. We accepted their invitation and came back a year later - when we were met by the Mayor and taken to lunch. We raced the following day around the streets of Dieppe. We encountered cobblestones, steep hills and sprint tactics which was all new for us being more familiar with long breakaways. Still we acquitted ourselves fairly well finishing in the first twenty though not in the first few.

There was a rather unexpected bonus to come. After the race we were invited to dinner and afterwards to the Grand Bal. At the "Grand Bal" delightful young ladies were queuing up to dance with us, there were obviously advantages to being a racing cyclist in France to the UK. We were always amazed by our reception where ever we went in France where racing cyclists were heroes.

On our trips to France we would ride 100 miles or more each day. Being on a limited budget we often slept rough in dry ditches – which were warmer than haystacks. On the nights spent in small hotels food was always accompanied by unlabeled bottles of wine. Omelettes were a firm favourite. Heading south we would get high in to the Alps but never quite made the Mediterranean.

After two years touring France one of our number said let's go to Spain. The war had not been over that long and Spain was still recovering from its vicious civil war. It was an outrageous decision, everybody said we must be mad. Undeterred we began organizing the trip. One of our group of 6 would learn Spanish, another who was at London University would contact the embassy to arrange the necessary visas. We also had to get a bond to ensure that we did not sell our bicycles while in Spain! Another would plan routes and try to get maps. I undertook to be the mechanic with a tool kit, spare spokes etc.

All went to plan: we cycled to Dover then on to Paris where we took a train – third class to Carcassonne North of the Pyrenees. From Carcassonne we cycled to the Pyrenees and in to Andorra. There was only a semi dirt road with a wooden customs post. The customs officials were very friendly and asked us to race among ourselves over the high pass. They went ahead in a vehicle and put a line across the road. We duly obliged and it was good sport to race up round the hair pin bends to the top. I suspect they were placing bets. When we returned the following day after staying in Andorra the night the customs officials invited us in for a glass of wine. At that time you could not go from Andorra in to Spain.

Customs post in to Andorra 1949

We then cycled along the French side of the Pyrenees to the Mediterranean where we went to a small town where one could get in to Spain. From here we cycled along the Spanish side of the Pyrenees to a small town La Seu d' Urgell. Here we decided to stop at a grand old fashioned hotel. That night we decided to splash out financially and have a really good meal. A small barrel of wine on the table and excellent food – cigars for the smokers. When our only Spanish speaker settled the bill in the morning he said it came to £1.50. We said that's not bad, £1.50 each. He said, no that is for all of us. Spain was ridiculously cheap.

From here the inland journey to Barcelona crossed a very arid region. It was very hot indeed and the roads were little more than dirt tracks. At one point a bridge over a river had been blown up in the civil war and we had to follow a track, wade the river to come out the other side. It was too hot to cycle after 11 in the morning

until round three in the afternoon.
Eventually we reached Barcelona where we stayed for a couple of days and went to a bull fight. We then commenced our return journey on the Costa Brava on the Mediterranean coast. The road was very rough and we had something like twenty punctures before getting to the border. There was virtually no where to stay, there being just small fishing villages. The only accommodation was small primitive guest houses. I have not been back but understand it is now solid with holiday resorts and hotels.

Returning we stopped at a small border town Port-Bou. In the evening we went to an open air dance in the town square. I asked a very pretty girl to dance, using my very limited French. She agreed and we chatted in French, rather badly and hesitantly. After about 10minutes we found out we were both English.
Back to Carcassonne and home, another great adventure.

Meantime my racing cycling had gathered momentum. Our most serious efforts went in to the mass start "road racing". This was held in summer on disused aerodromes, parks, or private circuits. By this time I knew I was at my best when up against others using tactics rather than riding against the clock. I was fortunate having a team mate – Bernard Harris - who was a better rider than me and a third member of the team – Jim Greaves – who was obsessively dedicated to the sport. We made a very competitive team.

Our team entries were always accepted for the classic

races, including the world championship selection race, the Olympic team selection, the first open road race. We always acquitted ourselves well although not quite good enough to get on the podium.

Warwick cyclo cross

A few high lights for this Rugby racing club team: equal first 1952 national road race at Birkenhead Park; in the bunch at four hours thirty-seven minutes for world

National Cyclist's Union

presents

THE FIRST

LONDON–LEAMINGTON

CYCLE ROAD RACE

(Under N.C.U. Rules)

Distance : 84 miles

Saturday, 5th July, 1952

Starting at 1 p.m.

from

Kensington Borough Playing Fields

Western Avenue, Northolt

A Famous Film Actress will Start the Race

See Gt. Britain's International
and 1952 Olympic Riders

Official Programme - - Sixpence

W. A. Webb. Printer, 22, Northfield Ave., West Ealing, W.13. Tel.: Ealing 1627.

championship selection; being among the one hundred riders chosen to participate in the mass start road race in England (the national police having granted permission for a limited number to race from London to Leamington). Both Bernard Harris and myself finished this race well up the field.

Road racing at Blenheim Palace

One of my best performances was when I broke away from the main bunch on my own in a hundred mile classic road race to select a team for the world championships. I was joined by Bob Maitland, the National Champion, with only five miles to go. He said "Come on, its in the bag." Taking turns at the front doing "bit and bit", however the pace was too much for me and I was completely burnt out before the finish and had to watch the main bunch go past me. After the race Bob Maitland came to me, shook my hand and said why didn't I just sit on his back wheel and I would have been second.

Another big race was at Blenheim palace on Whit-Monday. This race was a hundred kilometres on a narrow tarmac road. There were several climbs including a one in four gradient. Because of the dangers of the circuit with a hundred riders we made the unlikely decision as a team to go flat out from the start. This would thin the field and make it safer for us. This we did to devastating effect because nobody was willing to take up the chase that early in the race. There was a very big crowd at the finish and the end of the race was very exciting. We had been "away" the whole race but the bunch was chasing hard with one lap to go. We were first over the line with the bunch close behind. It had been a very exciting race but I took a real beating at the end. When I looked at my back wheel after the race it was as if it had been sprayed with aluminium paint. The quick release hollow spindle had broken and had been running on the casing.

Our greatest achievement as a team was the Isle of Man International Race of hundred-and-thirteen and three-quarter mile race – three times around the Island. It was the most prestigious race in the UK and attracted riders from all over the world, including top European riders.

England had put in 3 teams of 4 riders, but none of us had been selected. Whilst I did not think I was good enough to be selected my team mate Bernard Harris should have been, a grave injustice but ultimately to our advantage.

At the club AGM it was proposed that if our team was good enough to be selected for the Isle of Man then the club would pay our travelling expenses but not our accommodation. The president of our club, the owner of a big cycle shop who was critical of our way of life, said he would vote yes because he did not think the teams entry would be accepted. He was wrong as our entry was accepted.

Due to our previous performances we decided to ride in the National Championships at Birkenhead Park Liverpool on the Saturday prior to the Isle of Man race. We were able to combine the two racing at Birkenhead to finish equal first before embarking on the ferry to race on the Thursday at the Isle of Man.

We stopped in a small guesthouse in Douglas on the Isle of Man where the residents became enthusiastic about our team. The owner of the guesthouse managed to get us a pound of raisins for sustenance during the race. Remember some foods were still restricted although the war had finished seven years previously.

MANX INTERNATIONAL, VIKING TROPHY and MANNIN VEG
BICYCLE RACES

THURSDAY, JUNE 26th, 1952

Over the Tourist Trophy Course, Isle of Man

MASSED STARTS at 11 a.m., 11-35 a.m. and 2 p.m.

[Photo : F. Slemen, Liverpool]

Organised by the Manx Viking Wheelers' Cycling Club in conjunction with the Douglas June Effort and Season Extension Committee, and held under N.C.U. Rules.

Hon. Race Secretary: J. CURWEN CLAGUE, "Berwyn," Port-e-Chee Avenue, Douglas, Isle of Man.

ENTRIES CLOSE—Saturday, May 31st, 1952

We had two supporters from our club to help but were surprised when we were having our bikes checked to meet an enthusiast from Rugby who had taken a weeks holiday to watch the race. We did not know him but he had followed our performances and said the team award was within our reach. We humoured and thanked him but laughed when he had gone at his ridiculous suggestion. Amongst other international teams the French and Italians were there with their own mechanics and chefs. There were also the English A, B and C teams. What chance did we have?

On the big day the riders all walked with their bikes in front of the grandstand whilst their national anthems were played. We shambled along behind.

Off we went and we soon lost sight of our team mate Jim, but Bernard and I stuck together as the field thinned. We climbed the mountain for the first time to descend at a recorded 52 miles per hour. This was the first time electronic timing was used. We were both settled now and realized there was plenty of time. On the second circuit we were in the main bunch on a smaller hill and my team mate broke away and the peloton did not follow. I realized he was testing the reluctance of the peloton to chase. On the third time round he repeated the process, taking me with him. We were away although there were exceptional riders already ahead of us.

We were still away from the main bunch when we hit the mountain for the third time. My team mate dropped me on the final climb and I could not understand when our team supporters were going berserk when I came over the top. I pushed hard down the mountain for the third time, overtaking two riders on the steep descent to sprint for the finish. I thought we had done well to finish in such a tough and prestigious race. I was recovering from the ride when suddenly our unknown team supporter emerged shouting "You've won the team, what did I tell you"! Our third member had come in sprinting with the main bunch.

There was a dinner for the riders where the Governor of the island presented us with a shield having a solid silver profile of the Isle of Man.

On returning in triumph with our trophy the president said he would put it in his shop window. We said ok but only after it has been in the pub for a week.

The year 1952 had been an exceptional one in my cycle racing career. I had met Joan, a member of the cycling club, and we were to get married. Married life and racing were unlikely to mix so I decided to concentrate on married life and my career.

Cyclists' Great Riding

Bernard Harris (*Turbine Winding*), and Jim Grieves, (*Tool Room*), both members of the BTH Recreation Club Cycling Section along with A. J. Bailey, recently put up a brilliant performance to carry off two of the major team events of the season when riding for the Rugby R.C.C.

In the 114-mile Isle of Man International Race over the T.T. course they rode with skill and determination to win the Sun Challenge Trophy against stiff competition from France, Belgium, Holland, Canada, South Africa and New Zealand, as well as the British Isles. Their other important success was in the National Championship Mass Start at Birkenhead five days earlier, when they were awarded joint first place.

Although the Midlands is regarded as the home of mass start cycling the Sun Challenge Trophy had never previously been won by a Midland Club, and has in fact only once previously been south of Yorkshire, in 1946, when it was taken to France by the Velo Club de Paris. The presentation to the Rugby team was made by the Governor of the Isle of Man.

Bernard Harris (left) and Jim Grieves with the Sun Challenge Trophy which they won when competing with A. J. Bailey for the Isle of Man International Cycle Race.

CHAPTER 8

Family Life

In the early days of our courtship Joan's father was tragically killed in a motor cycling accident. She was academically very bright and had an exceptionally good school leaving certificate, which would have ensured her a university place but the economics now that her mother was widowed prevented this.

My life had changed. I was now twenty-five and I decided to give up serious cycle racing and concentrate on our relationship with a view to getting married. I was working for the Austin motor company and living part time in Birmingham. I decided to apply for a post in Coventry so that I could live in Rugby and see more of Joan and save some money.

Having accepted a job with Alvis in Coventry I was able to live at home and travel to Coventry daily by bus. My next move was to purchase a motor car. I eventually bought a 1935 Austin Ruby Saloon, with sun roof, fixed starting handle and a platform at the back for luggage. It cost £25. It had been around the clock and done over 100,000 miles. However using my engineering skills I worked on it, virtually rebuilding it, then I painted it red and black with normal house hold paint. It enabled Joan and me to search for a house and have some social excursions, as well as giving me a means of getting to work.

Before getting married we decided to go on an adventure with the car which was by this time in very good condition and I knew it intimately. I had spent many hours replacing and repairing parts and had complete confidence that all would be well if we took an ambitious trip – I even had a spare connecting rod with a new white metal bearing, confident that I could replace it at the roadside in the event of failure. I think I would rather cross Africa in a Ruby Saloon than in modern cars with their remarkable sophistication.

After investigation we decided that a sensible trip would be to go to France and explore the Vosges mountains of Alsace Lorraine. The reason for choosing this area was that it was said to be similar to our own Lake district with rounded mountains known as "Ballons" and had been the scene of invasion by Germany in the second world war. It was also relatively close to the UK thus keeping motoring to a minimum. This area of France was then very undeveloped with half timbered buildings, it was at one time part of Germany and close to the Rhine river.

It was a gastronomic experience for us both. One exceptional and memorable meal was when we stopped the night at a small inn. We were welcomed by a rotund and jolly lady who said dinner would be ready at 7pm. We sat in the bar, there was no menu. Initially we were presented with a huge tureen of soup and a bottle of red and a bottle of white wine, both without labels. We said to our hostess we would like to try a bottle of region, she rushed away and came back with a bottle of Alsace

Riesling and two wine glasses with long green stems. She poured with great reverence; it was excellent and she smiled when we expressed our delight.

The next course was trout, which she explained had been caught in a local stream that day. They were presented twisted on a bed of mashed potatoes, with a red berry of some kind in their eyes. Next we had pork with globe artichokes. The whole meal was completed with a splendid cheese board and brandy. When I came to pay the bill in the morning it was ridiculously cheap. I thanked her profusely and she gave me a great hug and said we must come back again. We never did return, but I remember the meal as one of the greatest in my life, perhaps enhanced by the years of wartime austerity in England.

Things went so well we pressed on to Switzerland, including crossing the Susten Pass which had several inches of snow on the top. Our brakes were smoking on the way down and the on coming traffic flashed lights at us. The Swiss were very friendly and delighted to see the vintage car. At one hotel by Lake Lucerne they said we need not pay for the second night of our stay because the manager was so impressed by our adventure. The whole staff including the chef came out to wave us farewell and take photographs.

1935 Austin Ruby Saloon De-Lux - with sun roof – negotiating the Susten Pass in Switzerland.

We kept the car after we married and moved to Berkswell. It completed another 25,000 miles before we sold it for £25 to replace it with a new Ford Anglia. The Ruby Saloon had enabled us to search for a suitable property to purchase and renovate.

We had saved sufficient money before getting married to obtain a mortgage. We agreed that we would like to find an old, possibly half timbered , property in the country. Having spent nearly a year driving round in the Ruby Saloon looking we had not found one that suited our requirements. In desperation we decided to purchase a plot of land, I would design a house and subcontract the building of it. The plan was to live in the house and eventually sell it at a profit.

The second place we looked at was in Berkswell. We had to look at a map to find where Berkswell was. We located the plot, which was overgrown with fallen trees, nettles and brambles, but agreed it would do. When I talked to my colleague at work he said "Tell the estate agent you will have it subject to contract. This means you can always pull out if you find a problem." This was useful advice but after examining the plot in detail, including digging test holes, all appeared to be well. We established that it was once the vegetable garden of the old rectory.

I drew the plans, found a builder and obtained planning permission. It was very easy to get a building society loan because we had saved about thirty per cent of the cost and my salary was regarded as substantial.

Then we hit the first problem. Because the land had belonged to the church a condition of purchase was that the plans were approved by the Parochial Church Council. Other clauses included not complaining about bell ringing and putting in stock proof boundary fences. The Berkswell estate was owned by the Wheatley family who lived at Berkswell Hall. Affairs in the village had been dominated by the lords of the manor of Berkswell since Norman times. In accordance to this tradition Mrs Wheatley was chairperson of the parochial council and she said she did not like the colour of the tiles. Therefore she did not give approval for the plans.

We thought there was no alternative to brown and a little research found that we could appeal to the Bishop of Coventry on decisions made by parochial councils. Out of decency I decided to tell the rector of our decision to appeal. When I visited him he was in the new rectory on the Meriden road in his study wearing a black cloak. When I told him of our decision he whirled around the room saying don't do this – he reminded me of a wounded crow. Next day he contacted me and said all right you can have brown tiles. I thanked him profusely and we were able to commence building, realizing that we were the first to build in Berkswell for about a hundred years.

Whilst the house was being built we cleared the land and tidied up the hedges. I would dig the land for about two hours a day, and when the blisters hardened I enjoyed the pioneering spirit.

One problem that arose was that of moles. There were mole hills everywhere. By this time I had become acquainted with some of the villagers who gave me a crash course on how to catch moles. The offensive was successful and I had heard that a moleskin waist coat would be a rather special item of country clothing. I determined to nail out the moleskins, dry them and get them cured. Believe me that there is nothing worse than the smell of a mole's skin. I was delighted when I heard that moleskin was a type of cloth. In any case I did not like catching them, perhaps because of "Wind in the Willows" and even now I do not do anything about moles in the garden – I like moles.

Once we were married and living in the new house there was a lot to do. I would work most evenings building shelves and cupboards through out the house. We both enjoyed the garden and became virtually self sufficient in vegetables and fruit. I also changed the sewerage from a cess pit to the newly constructed sewerage mains system. This was a formidable task because of the number of springs encountered which kept filling the trench with water. I was struggling with this when the local policeman cycled past. He offered to help, we successfully completed the job and we became life long friends.

One of the highlights of these early summers was to purchase a five gallon barrel of cider at a ridiculously low price. This meant that cider was only four pence a pint, say two pence in new money. The problem was that once broached you had to drink the barrel before it went off. You had to enlist friends to come and help you drink it. On one occasion I was about to drive in the wooden tap, having removed my trousers to prevent them being soaked in cider if I was unable to get the tap in quickly. There was a knock on the door, it was one of Joan's friends so I shut the pantry door and was trapped trouser-less with the cider for what seemed a very long time.

I still retained my shooting interest and would visit my cousin's farm where his working terriers were delighted to see me. Gradually Joan and I became friends with the Berkswell farmers. One of our farmer friends suggested I had a word with the Berkswell Estate's game keeper to see if he would let me join in pigeon shooting at the end of the pheasant shooting season. One very cold night I walked to the keeper's cottage in the middle of the Berkswell Estate to enquire about the pigeon shooting. The head keeper said they would not be doing any pigeon shooting that year. However early in February I heard lots of shooting and planned my response. The following winter I fed the garden with grain and reaped my revenge by shooting pheasants with a .410 out of the window.

Eventually I got to know the keeper and was able to shoot pigeons on the Estate. I also helped the game keeper by beating. One of the highlights was the Christmas shoot, where the "guns" shot until around 2pm then finished the day with a splendid lunch and drinks in the keeper's house. The beaters would have their lunch in an outside building but the guns always sent out bottles of whisky.

The assistant keeper who was reputed to have been a muleteer in Wingate's Chindits army in Burma during World War 2 could not resist the temptation of the whisky and rapidly became legless. The problem was how to get him home? The solution, a wheelbarrow. He was taken home and left in the barrow on the doorstep, his friends having knocked on the door and rapidly disappeared.

It was not long before our first child was due to be born. Jane was born in a maternity hospital near Coleshill. Although perfectly well Joan was there for a week and even then when she came home current custom meant that she stayed in bed another week whilst a local woman came in to cook and clean for us.

When our second child was due there was a midwife living less than a hundred yards away and we planned for Joan to stay at home this time. The midwife was insistent that when the birth was immanent she should be phoned. On no account was I to go and knock on the door. This meant I had to go to the phone box which was much further away up by the Bear Inn!

Life was good, I was doing well at work and our two children were happy at the village school. We had a small broken coated terrier, Poppy. Two fields up from our house was a pond full of crucian carp, these fish were most obliging and easily caught by the village children who would assemble at the pond in the summer evenings with their rods. No television in those days but real fun. The idea of selling the house had long since disappeared.

Jane and Tom

Poppy the dog joined in all our activities with great enthusiasm. One of my friends, a local builder who was also the undertaker, would come with me and Poppy each Saturday to go pigeon shooting. By this time farmers were more than happy to have us come and shoot pigeons who were decimating their crops. Using decoys we would shoot up to a hundred pigeons in a day. These we would store in an old deep freeze to be collected by a butcher who exported them to France. The price we obtained meant we were running at a profit and could occasionally take our wives out to dinner on the proceeds.

One day I was on my way to the village shop when I met a funeral procession which was on foot being led by my shooting friend. The dog recognized him and leapt in the air with joy – to Jim's credit he never blinked an eyelid and proceeded to the church with a dog leaping round his feet.

For good pigeon shooting you have to locate where they are feeding. Jim had a local funeral and instructed the driver of the hearse to go a long way round from the church to the cemetery so that he could view a field of oil seed rape where he thought the pigeons might be feeding. At the wake after the funeral, the deceased's daughter came to Jim and thanked him profusely. She wanted to know how Jim knew of the house where the mother had been born and had taken the long route to go past it. She thought she was the only person with that knowledge. Jim just nodded.

Every year we would load up the car with camping equipment, take the ferry and motor across France, stopping at remote campsites. The children grew up, Jane trained as a nurse, Tom had a place at Solihull Sixth Form College to study engineering. It was then that Joan was diagnosed with an inoperable liver cancer. With Jane and her friend's help Joan was able to stay at home where she died six months later.

CHAPTER 9

MOUNTAINS

Annapurna Circuit, Everest, Kilimanjaro, Mt Kenya, Birmingham University Fell Walkers, Ben Nevis, Stok Kangri, Mera Peak, Italian Dolomites, Peru, K2, Frozen Zanskar River

I was 52 when Joan died and needed to readjust my life. Jane had left home and Tom decided to live at home while taking an engineering degree at Coventry university.

At this time I was chief engineer of the machinery division at Massey Ferguson, an interesting but demanding job. What was I to do? Well meaning friends introduced me to widows and single ladies. However I did not wish to settle and began to look around for new interests and new friends. To this end I joined a badminton club in Solihull where nobody knew me or my background. Two younger men in the club said they were divers and invited me to join them on a trip to the Red sea. As I was considering this idea I picked up a mountaineering magazine . Amongst the advertisements was an organized trip in the Himalayas, the Annapurna circuit in Nepal. This appealed to me more than the diving even though my friends thought I was mad. They said I would find it too difficult and the people who went on high altitude trips were younger and fitter than me.

Undeterred, I bought some boots, socks, ruck sack etc. and read some books on the subject. I ran seven miles twice a week and went on long walks every weekend, mainly in the Cotswolds. One day in summer I decided to walk from first light to dusk in the Cotswolds; at dusk I could see the lights of Winchcombe where I had left my car. So I sat down and ate an orange. When I came to get going again I could hardly move but eventually stumbled into Winchcombe. A lesson on pushing myself to the limit.

My first expedition was the Annapurna circuit leaving in October. At the airport I made friends with a small Londoner who was president of a London walking club. Dennis and I got on well and agreed we would share a two man tent for the next three weeks. An important decision when you are going to face adversity.

We arrived at Katmandu and spent a couple of days looking at Temples and other sights. There were very few powered vehicles around but you could readily travel on bicycle rickshaws.

Annapurna circuit at the lower levels children in the villages would always view us with great curiosity.

Eventually our party of twelve got underway. The first problem was that we caught the tail end of the monsoon, experiencing huge warm rain drops which soon soaked everything in our small two man tents.

After a couple of days when we were camping in a small village the skies suddenly cleared and we had a memorable and incredible view of the Himalayas. It did not rain again the whole trip. I found I was able to cope well with the pace and nearly always accompanied a strong walker, younger than myself, who owned a sports shop in Norwich. We climbed steadily but when we reached the snow line the porters deserted us.

To be fair some of the porters had never been in snow. Although we had bought them cheap plastic sandals they had sold these long before and were reluctant to go high. One porter however did stay with us but his feet were so badly frost bitten when we descended from the high mountains he could not walk or carry a load. The Sherpa boss, Sidar, dismissed him without further pay and he was therefore unable to get home. When our group said we would have a whip round to finance his return by a low route the Sidar was emphatic we should not do this otherwise we would be taken for granted and exploited. The Sidar did however say it was ok to give the lame porter cigarettes. What he did not know was that concealed in the cigarette packets there were enough notes for the porter to get home.

When the porters left us we were reluctant to turn back. We abandoned all but the absolute essentials – first aid kit, some cooking equipment and fuel were left behind. We were to live on rice for the next 2 weeks. Our Sherpa guides, as opposed to the porters, remained loyal and carried increased loads. Eventually we climbed the highest point, a pass at 18,000 feet. Some of the party were suffering from altitude sickness and I noticed my friend from the sports shop was missing. On reaching the highest point and asking where he was I was told he was having a rest. Getting one of the group to look after my

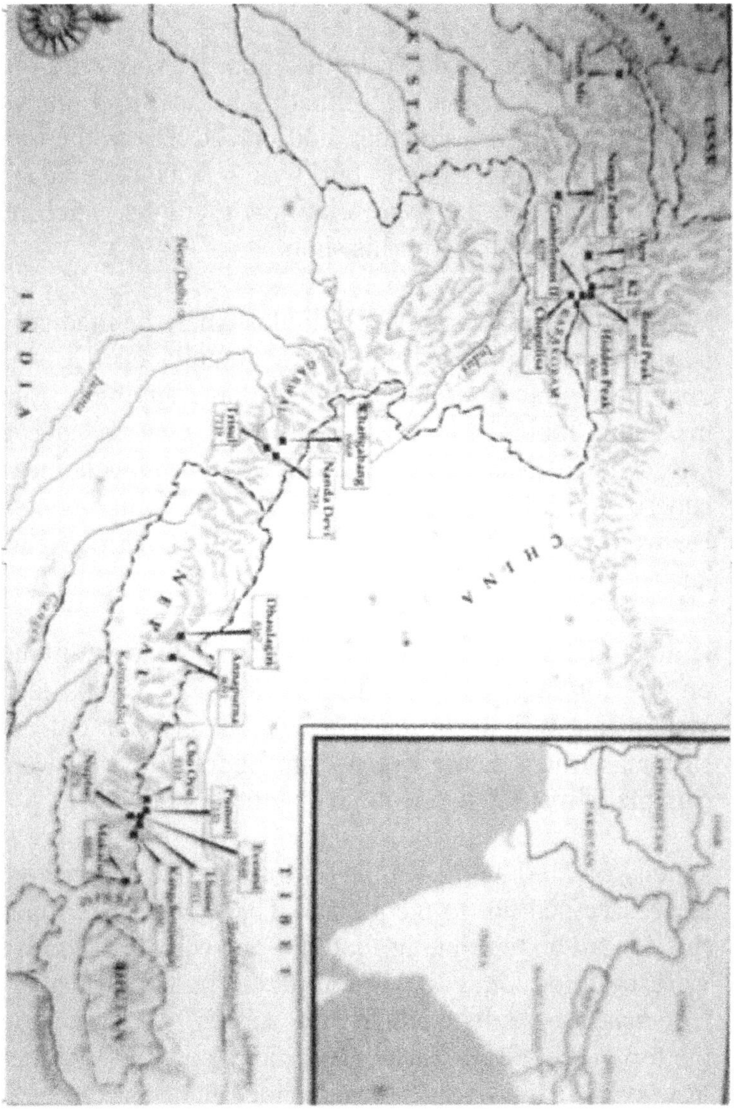
INDIA
NEPAL
CHINA
TIBET

ruck sack I returned down to find him, he was suffering from altitude sickness. I took his ruck sack, told him to put his hand on my shoulder, and nursed him to the top. He produced his camera but was too bewildered to operate it; I took the appropriate photographs which he was desperate to have for his shop.

We then descended to lower altitudes where he gradually became more coherent and was eventually ok. He was extremely grateful and said I could have anything from his shop. Jokingly I said it would be great to have a goose down jacket at cost price. On returning home a superb goose down jacket arrived with his compliments . He would not accept payment of any kind. Thirty years later the jacket is still in use.

If anybody wishes to loose weight they could try living on rice for twenty days and climb to about 18,000 feet. We all lost weight on the trip but the Sherpa's did not suffer as much as we did. I think their stomachs were capable of making use of huge quantities of rice.

When you are hungry you begin to fantasize about food, so we decided not to mention it. There was a ten rupee fine for anybody bringing food into the conversation. We were trudging along at high altitude one day when my tent mate suddenly produced ten rupees and shouted at the top of his voice, "Steak and kidney pudding with lots of gravy." It was then that we decided it would be better to order the next meal – you were not going to get it, but it was far more fun than suppression. One day my selection was as follows: gin and tonic with ice and lemon, langoustine in a garlic sauce with a crisp German Riesling, fillet steak with new potatoes and garden peas with Chateau Neuf du Pape , crème caramel, a ripe Roquefort cheese to finish with port, coffee brandy and walnuts to finish. My friend said my word Bill that sounds good, I think I'll order the same. We finished up as usual with rice.

As we were descending from the Annapurna circuit we decided we would purchase a goat for the team to eat. The goat was slaughtered in due course but I noticed the Sherpa's were only eating the liver. I joined them and the liver was excellent. The rest of the party eating the rest of the goat found it very tough, virtually inedible despite their hunger.

Although the expedition was tough - I lost over a stone in weight, such that people did not recognize me on my return – I was hooked. This was my thing, the big mountains. The following year I signed on for a top graded expedition to Kala Pattar above Everest base camp, taking in the Gokyo Lakes and the Khumbu glacier. Possibly the most uncanny story of this expedition was the discovery of the special aero engine I had worked on 25 years previously on the air strip at Luckla (see Alvis chapter).

However another uncanny story was that of a dog. On landing at Luckla and setting out a black and white thick coated medium sized husky type dog decided to accompany us. Some members of the party threw stones at it but it was clear that it was determined to come with us. If the path forked and you had lost sight of the group, perhaps because you had stopped to photograph, it would wait for you and show you the way. It slept outside our tents even in snow. We became attached to it and fed it a few scraps.

Our unexpected guide at high altitude

At about 18,000 feet I developed a cold, from my tent mate who had just recovered! Our leader decided that he did not want the whole group to become infected and proposed that I should not tackle the high snow covered pass but take a much further route sleeping in the Sherpa's' hut over night and re-join the party after two days. He provided me with a Sherpa as a guide and all went according to plan. On leaving the Sherpa's hut the following morning, with half a day's walking to catch up with the main party, I was surprised to see the dog trotting down the path towards me. When it saw me it was overjoyed and immediately turned around from whence it had come to lead me on a three hour walk to join the others. On meeting the main group I told them the story and one member said he had left his tent to answer the call of nature and was surprised when he saw the dog leaving camp. The dog accompanied us for the rest of the journey and the last we saw of it was sitting beside the runway as we took off. Was it waiting for another group to look after in the mountains?

Another unusual experience for me on this expedition was when, at high altitude, I listened to Elgar's cello concerto. It was common practice to climb in the morning and return to a slightly lower altitude for an afternoon nap, this being part of the acclimatization process before tackling a summit. On this particular day we camped at an outstandingly beautiful spot surrounded by snow covered peaks. Although the rest of the party retired to their tents for their nap I decided to stop outside. My tent mate had offered me his Walkman which I had accepted with no intention of using it. The silence and beauty of the peaks was incredible and, out of curiosity, I switched on the Walkman to be immediately entranced by the music. I felt as if I had been drugged and the combination of clear air, high altitude, the peaks and Elgar had an effect on me that I have never been able to repeat.

This trip was a tough one so the following year I decided to go on an easier expedition, Mount Kenya and

Kilimanjaro in Africa. Mount Kenya was tackled first which gave useful acclimatization. The ability to cope with altitude however is not totally dependent on fitness. There was one younger member of the party who really suffered despite having had a rigorous fitness program before he came. My advice to him was to go slowly, be last and prepare by walking many miles up hill. I was able to climb Kilimanjaro, a 6,000 metre peak without too much trouble and more important descend quickly to get to the hut where there were only one or two bottles of beer!

Relaxing in a game park after climbing **Mt Kilimanjaro and Mt Kenya.**

It was on this African trip that I met Ken Dickinson. He was the Birmingham University doctor and we rapidly became good friends. It was he, who on our return, invited me to join the Birmingham University Fell Walking Club. For me this was another break through.

Once a month the university would organize a bus, leaving at 7am in the morning. It would go to English mountain areas such as the Lakes and Wales for day trips. They also organized camping weekends away, going further a field including the Scottish mountains. I rapidly became involved socially as well.

My preference was to go scrambling, climbing up mountain routes without ropes. In some ways this is more dangerous than climbing with protection as it was often a long way down if you slipped. On one scrambling expedition I teamed up with another member of the university and we set off to tackle a rather indistinctive route. On reaching a ledge, a critical point on the climb, we were not certain of the route. I volunteered to climb up to investigate. The route proved to be impossible so I asked my companion to talk me down. It is easier to climb up than down because you cannot see the footholds when coming down. What I had forgotten was that my climbing friend stuttered when excited and when he tried to instruct me he began stuttering badly such that he was incoherent and I could not decide what foot he wanted where......when I eventually got down his speech returned to normal.

It was about this time that I wanted to improve my mountain skills. I heard that the Ben Nevis mountain rescue team would take one or two people with them over the New Year period. The candidates would be involved in team practice of techniques and, if there was a need, in a real rescue. I rang the leader, an ex marine commando, and discussed the proposal, pointing out that

I was now in my late 50's. To which he replied that if I was not up to it he would simply send me home.

Off I went on Boxing day driving up to the snow clad Scottish mountains, taking a bottle of whiskey with me as a good will gesture. I got on well with the team and did some interesting navigation and map reading practice culminating in being dropped off individually from a Land-Rover in wild country, not knowing exactly where you were and having to find your way back to base. Whist I coped well with map and compass it was this experience that inspired me to design a plastic gadget to make navigation easier. Subsequently, through my work colleagues, I patented and marketed this device. I sold a fair number and the army did contact me as they found the device invaluable on Dartmoor where they frequently lost people. Sat-navs have since reduced the need for such aids.

The experience with the Ben Nevis mountain rescue was excellent and included lowering people on stretches over cliffs and ice axe techniques. One day our leader emphasized that one should always expect the unexpected. We were all on a steep snow covered slope and he singled me out and said crouch down facing the slope. This I did expecting a demonstration but he simply pushed me over and it was some time before I brought myself to a stop with my ice axe. A useful tip that probably saved my life on a later Himalayan expedition.

The highlight of the week was when the leader presented

me with two short handled climbing axes. We trekked in

On Ben Nevis with the mountain rescue team

to the valley below Ben Nevis and looked at the formidable ice and snow covered gullies. The weather was reasonable although snowing slightly when we started out. With the aid of ropes, crampons and two short climbing axes we started to scale a gulley thinking we were practising front pointing and would turn back after a short time. No way were we going to the top. However we reached the top and the weather changed, it was a white-out, you could not read or hold a map or compass. Our leader, cupping his hand and shouting into each individual's ear told us we were going to rope up there and go down the edge of the mountain, it being the best way to get out of a dangerous situation. This we did, one moment sheet ice, the next deep snow. Eventually, after slipping over and having to use ice axes to stop, then being up to our waists in snow, the clouds cleared and we realized we were not going to die that day. At that time Ben Nevis was the number two killer in the world

I learnt a lot in a week and went again the following year. The leader said I was the only person to come back to train a second time with the mountain rescue. Everybody else thought one week was enough. Whilst with this group we did a little exercise and slept overnight in snow bothy. To carry the coal, whisky, food and so on we were provided with huge rucksacks. I thought I was being clever when I fluffed up my rucksack with a jersey. However when the leader picked up my rucksack he said good you can carry the coal. When I explained that I could not lift it on to my back he said, sit on a chair and we will help you to your feet, all you have to do is walk.

It was on this trip that one of our group fell in to a stream that was only partially frozen. The leader said to the victim, take all your clothes off, which he did despite the icy wind, and we were all asked to contribute one item of clothing. This we did and after about 10 minutes he stopped shaking. Another exercise was to dig a snow hole and sleep in it. Because we were able to start early while still light the snow hole proved to be surprisingly effective. It was a very useful lesson on survival and showed clearly that you must make your judgments early if you are not going to make your destination. Prepare your snow hole before you are exhausted and it is still light to see where and how to locate it.

One final point about the mountain rescue team was that they relished the challenge of a rescue. When we were in the pub and the phone rang they would call "Is it a shout", the term used for a phone call that somebody was lost on the Ben and there was a need for immediate action. Rescues were not always successful and bodies were often not located until the spring. The crows found them first. On one occasion an indignant watcher wrote to the local paper and complained that the mountain rescue had not treated a body with adequate respect, simply putting a corpse in a body bag and letting it slide freely down the mountain over the snow. There was a letter the following week from the mountain rescue inviting the letter writer to join them and risk his life accompanying a body off the mountain – there was no further correspondence. The experience and training in Scotland was to prove invaluable for me on later expeditions.

One year I teamed up with Richard whom I had got to know on my second Himalayan expedition in the Everest and Kala Patar region. We decided to tackle another 6,000 metre peak, Stok Kangri, which is near to Leh in Kashmir. To acclimatize we joined a trekking group doing a circuit with a pass of 5,000 metres in Kashmir. This was a reasonable trek and although some of the group suffered altitude sickness. One problem was though that the porters used ponies instead of yaks and two of the ponies died on the high pass. The vultures, lammergeyers, arrived as we started to descend.

Stok Kangri photographed with my OM10. Despite trying to keep weight to a minimum I always took 2 camera bodies for reliability, a wide angle and a telescopic lens.

At the end of the trek we recruited two local guides who had ponies to set up a small base camp for us from where we could attempt Stok Kangri. We reached a suitable spot to set up our base camp just as it was getting dark when, out of the gloom a figure appeared. It was a New Zealander and he asked whether he could buy some food. It appeared that he had thought he could reach the top of a 6,000 metre peak without crampons, ice axe etc.

We fed him and fixed him up with a tent, he was extremely grateful and headed cheerfully back to the lower levels the next day. We were also pleased because if he had gone on we may have found a body.

The following day we set out and camped at the bottom of an ice fall from whence we could attempt the summit. We left at first light, our crampons and ice axes biting in to the frozen snow and reached the summit without serious problems. Somewhat elated and perhaps a bit light headed we descended and when at the top of a massive steep icefall we decided to stop and have a drink from our thermos flasks. Both the guide and I stepped on to the snow and took off sliding down the steep slope to eternity. The snow over the ice had softened slightly and underneath there was ice like glass. Not panicking I remembered all I had been taught by the mountain rescue and got my ice axe underneath my shoulder to get my weight on it. It was hopeless, the ice was glass hard, however looking behind me I could see a substantial rock sticking out behind me and I used the spade end to steer me to the rock and I came to an abrupt halt. The guide had done exactly the same thing and Richard was able to get a rope to us and all was well. We then roped up for the descent and encountered no further problems. I did however learn one thing. When I looked at the tracks in the snow I was surprised to see that they covered a very short distance, and in that time I had done a lot of thinking, it would have seemed a very long time had I kept sliding.

We could go home now, or at least we thought so. On

arrival at the small airport they said there would be no flights that day or in the foreseeable future because of fog. After making diverse enquiries we realized our only hope was to make several days journey over the mountains to Srinagar and from there we could almost certainly get a train to Delhi. Eventually we found a man with a car who was prepared to take us over the mountains to Srinagar. The vehicle was in a pretty rough state - although there was no tread on the tyres the canvas was not actually showing through.

No choice. Off we went stopping overnight in simple huts. The food was less than basic, always being red beans with curry powder. However we were proceeding reasonably well when we came up against a military road block. Kashmir is a disputed territory between India and Pakistan and there is an on-going war in that area. The soldier at the road block was very polite but said we could go no further. I asked who was in charge and he pointed to a bungalow on the hill and then offered to escort us to see the officer in charge. When we arrived the officer emerged in his pyjamas. I promptly saluted him, shook hands and explained our predicament. He had impeccable English and explained that the road was mined and that he would let us through when it was clear. He had been to a public school in England and viewed us favourably. I thanked him profusely and saluted him again. He saluted me back and said you are a military man aren't you. I replied "Yes sir" ex military, the Warwickshire's. Excellent, he said, I thought so.
On our way back my colleague said you've never been in the army – but you are a very convincing liar.

We eventually arrived in Srinagar but there was gun fire in the streets. Srinagar is one of the most beautiful places in the world, with its lakes, mountains and house boats. We found a bed for the night on a house boat. After visiting the railway station and being refused tickets I found the right person to bribe. Richard was against bribery but finally agreed it was the only way out. It was a fifteen hour train journey to Delhi where, after a few days, we managed to get a flight home, three weeks later than planned. I had no problems with being late but for my friend, who was a surgeon, there must have been a lot of delayed facial operations in Manchester.

Mera Peak is possibly the highest Himalayan peak that can normally be climbed without oxygen. My surgeon friend Richard and I decided to have a crack at it and joined a small organized group. Whilst it was an advantage to have a medical man in the team the Sherpas became aware of his skills and there would always be a little queue at the small villages on our walk in. Sadly there were often cases which would have been dealt with easily in the UK but which in these inaccessible villages would be fatal.

On one occasion we were following a rather remote ascent and we came across a woman by the side of the trail indicating that she wanted medicines by pointing at her mouth. Richard followed her to a cave where her husband was lying on a blanket with a tooth abscess that according to Richard would almost certainly kill him. The jaw bone was rotten and he was in agony.

However Richard was of the opinion that he might survive if he was hit hard enough by antibiotics. Most of us carried some antibiotics of different types so we all contributed to a tin mug where the antibiotics were mashed up. Richard considered that he would not follow a course of antibiotics as instructed but he had the advantage of never having been subjected to antibiotics before, making them more effective. Did he survive? We never knew, we were to descend by a different route.

Mera Peak in the Himalayas

Our Mera group included a 24 year old Scot. He said that since he had been a small boy he had always wanted to climb a Himalayan peak. His family and friends had become so fed up with him talking about it they had had a whip around to finance the expedition. He was second in the Ben Nevis fell run which showed that he was a pretty tough character. He was however very sensible and asked me for advice. I simply said go slowly on the walk in, be last, and drink lots of water. However he could not resist the temptation to be up front and sadly I watched him deteriorate.

By the time we got to base camp I could see he was suffering badly. He was however remarkably determined and I advised him to take 5 steps and 5 deep breaths and repeat this on the final assault. I told him to leave his ruck sack behind and pick it up on the way down. But he had become somewhat incoherent. He made the top and we led him down but he never really recovered and seemed very fragile indeed when we boarded the aircraft for home. I often wondered whether he did himself permanent damage.

It was a magnificent climb. Ability to handle high altitude is a matter of luck although there are some useful guide lines. Climb slowly and gain altitude slowly, sometimes going higher then returning to camp at a slightly lower altitude and always drink lots of water, at least 6 pints a day. There was a diuretic tablet available called Diamox that helped some people but I never used it. The climb itself was not exceptionally difficult although it did require the use of ice axes, ropes and crampons. There were some intimidating crevasses and the possibility of avalanches.

Although the most significant expeditions were to the Himalayas I was always on the look out for less demanding climbing expeditions in Europe. We had a graduate working with us at Massey Ferguson and his French father in law was a guide in the French Alps. He suggested the three of us go on one of the higher, more difficult routes, hut-to-hut, in the Italian Dolomites. This required ropes, crampons and ice axes but there were ladders to link the ledges together. Some parts of the route were remnants of past military campaigns.

Climbing in the **Dolomites**

It was essential to be off the ladders by midday because there were vigorous electrical storms every afternoon. Where there were steel ladders, often covering several hundred feet, they were often twisted from lightening strikes. We found on the first attempt that we were the first through this spring and despite clearing ledges with our ice axes there was too much snow and ice to follow the highest route.

The mountain huts were open however and supplied by helicopter and managed by mountain guides who were pleased to see us and delighted to drink grappa with us. We went back the following year and completed the highest route hut to hutting. It was on this second expedition that we realized our guide from the Alps could not read a compass but insisted he was right against my compass and better judgment. Fortunately we met a small group of Italian mountain troops who had ropes and were able to get us back on the correct route. Obviously it is important to get to your next hut and not spend the night on the open mountains.

The Italian Dolomites are superb limestone mountains and especially attractive with cathedral like spires and solid rock. In all a remarkable experience.

My plan was now to sign up to a major expedition every year. The Cordillera Bianca mountain range in Peru provided my next adventure. Here our group met up with guides, who were essential because this was a time when the political bandits were very active and would shoot you for your boots. We flew in to Lima and travelled by bus on extremely rough roads with cracks where there had been earthquakes. It was along this west coast where a mud slide from the mountains had covered a complete town and only the church spire could be seen.

It was a very beautiful, wild area. There were lakes full of naïve trout that we were able to catch very easily to supplement our food supplies. All our camps were close but below the snow line, from where we would do minor expeditions following glaciers to higher altitudes. We were out for a month and used mules to carry our equipment. The book "Touching the Void" by Joe Simpson took place in this area. This was an incredible, true mountaineering story where a mountaineer had cut the rope of his companion to save his own life.

Peru – entertaining small children by singing "Down by the Station early in the morning…." which they enjoyed clapping along to despite not understanding a word of the song..

It was on the Peruvian trip that I met David Pearce, and we agreed that we would tackle the Baltoro glacier in

Pakistan to reach K2. This was considered a tough expedition taking over 5 weeks and a somewhat hazardous challenge. We flew in Skardu from Islamabad and were a little surprised to find a middle aged Scots lady join our group. She had faded and slightly worn equipment suggesting that she was an experienced mountain person. The route was somewhat unstable and at one place our porters said that they would not go forward if it rained because of the fear of avalanches. Fortunately it did not rain. The Baltoro is possibly the biggest glacier in the world being several miles wide and fed from several 8,000 metre peaks, including K2, Broad Peak and Masherbrum. The roar of the river before reaching the base of the glacier was continuous, like an express train. One of the unusual difficulties was obtaining drinking water. The water from the Baltoro river was grey with fine sediment and although I had taken some filter papers from our Massey Ferguson laboratories, which our lab people guaranteed would work, they did not. We had to rely on doubtful wells, and later, melted snow.

On reaching the foot of the glacier it was apparent the Scots woman was struggling and would not be able to cope with the tough conditions of altitude, cold and glacier ice. It was then we established the reason for her joining the expedition. Her son was a mountaineer and had been killed on the 8,000 metre Broad peak and she wanted to see where his body was. The Pakistani government would not retrieve his body and in any case it was too high for helicopters. The leader of our group had only accepted her on compassionate grounds, the faded equipment clearly had belonged to her son. She agreed she would not be able to go on so we planned to leave her with a tent, supplies and a porter at a pleasant spot before going up on to the ice. We would pick her up on our return. After fixing her camp David and myself climbed around and established and marked an accessible route where she could view Broad Peak.

The start of K2, a bridge made of twisted twigs.

The porters said their prayers and off we went to K2. One of the hazards was snow filled crevasses where porters had died on previous expeditions. We moved cautiously prodding the snow with sticks. Eventually we arrived where the glaciers forked often referred to as the throne of the mountain gods – you can see more 8,000 metre peaks than from anywhere else in the world. David and myself thought it a good idea to be first at this point so that we could get a good site to pitch our 2 man tent. This we did only to be told by our military guide that we could be shot at by Indian troops in this disputed area. We moved our tent!

Having established our base we set out the following morning while still dark to get to the K2 base camp. After several hours walking and scrambling the group leader and his assistant decided to turn around at Broad Peak base camp but we decided to press on and eventually reached the base 2 camp where we were rewarded by tea and biscuits. Time was running out for us and we headed back at maximum speed. On the way back it started to snow and we were pleased to see lights being waved at our camp to guide us across the ice gullies. On arrival I was very glad to creep in to my sleeping bag.

My friend David said I had taken a bit of a beating and I agreed but pointed out that I had had a mild stomach upset and had not eaten all day. You can get bugs on expeditions from the porters who have themselves become immune but are carriers. He pointed out gleefully that perhaps I was "past it." Revenge is sweet for when we descended a bug hit David with a vengeance and I had the joy of offering to carry his ruck sack and going ahead to setup our tent and even lay out his sleeping bag.

We had been to K2 so called because the mountain was so remote and inaccessible that the locals did not have a name for it and a British survey had given it the nominal name of K2 being short for Karakoram 2.

The Scottish lady we had left behind had climbed the route above her tent every morning and watched the sun rise over Broad Peak, where her son's body was. She was content with her achievement. It is worth remembering that deep frozen bodies retain eternal youth and will often turn up at the bottom of slow moving glaciers hundreds of years later.

On one of my trips I had met a mountain man who ran his own business organizing challenging expeditions. He was particularly interested in a winter exploration following the frozen Zanskar river to reach a remote village impossible to reach by land routes for 6 months of the year. It was understood that locals had completed this frozen river route in winter to obtain essentials. Not prepared to rely solely on locals he asked me to accompany him. I had been highly recommended by another mountaineer. Thinking that the river would be frozen and flat it seemed like a reasonable proposition. By some means he had persuaded or bribed the Indian military to pull us out by helicopter at the end of the gorge if we got in trouble.

I agreed to go and thought it a good idea to get some maps. I had a reliable source of specialist maps for previous expeditions but on this occasion the best they could find was a map made by a British survey team in 1928. The gorge that we were going to tackle was shown as not surveyed.

Zanskar River hot springs created amazing ice falls but in places weakened the ice dangerously on the main river.

Although we intended to take tents and climbing equipment it was rumoured that there might be some caves in which we could sleep. We flew in to a snow covered ice bound Leh. Electricity here was only available for part of the day. We found a small group of porters who had come down the frozen river and now wished to return to their village. We managed to bribe them to help us on our expedition.

We were driven part of the way to find our route blocked by an ice fall, increasing the length of our proposed trek. Finally we got to the frozen Zanskar river where it quickly emerged that it was not all going to be flat. Ice had thawed, and broken in slabs and re frozen creating piles of ice some 20 or 30 feet high. In other places the ice was flat with patches of open water, these warm patches were where the river was supplemented by hot springs, this being a volcanic region. The sides of the gorge were sheer in places and a minor avalanche high up the gorge would send a wave of ice and water down the gorge leaving no escape route. A rather depressing thought!

The locals we had recruited had very sturdy staves the purpose of which was to keep tapping the ice and by the sound establishing whether the ice would bear their weight. The water under the ice was going at high speed and if you were unfortunate enough to go through the ice that would be the end. The ice was of course very slippery and although I fitted my crampons it was difficult to walk any distance in them and they were rejected. In retrospect perhaps running spikes would have helped. Our porters had short military rubber boots which, whilst ok on the flat, were lethal when climbing. We often feared for their safety and marvelled at their apparent faith in the after life. My colleague had fortunately taken ropes, ice screws, climbing gear that enabled us to climb partway up out of the gorge enabling us to by pass some of the dangerous areas.

It was difficult to find flat places to camp. When we did find a cave in which to spend the night it meant sleeping at an angle crammed in with the porters as the caves were so small. Eventually, after about 14 days, we safely reached the end of the gorge. There were one or two isolated dwellings at that point where we had a party, drinking raw raksi (fermented millet) and singing songs. I sang "My old man's a dustman" which was enthusiastically received although they did not understand a word of it. They did however enjoy banging saucepan lids to the rhythm.

It was at this point that we discovered that only one porter was prepared to go back down the gorge. This made it impossible for both of us to go back. After discussion I agreed to trek two or three more days to a bigger village where I could be picked up by helicopter. These helicopters only had capacity for the pilot and one passenger, so one of us would have to trek back. Two porters were prepared to accompany me to their home village at the head of the gorge from where it was said to be possible to radio for a pre arranged helicopter to pick me up.

The walking was easier and safer now and after one overnight stay in a primitive dwelling, sleeping on the floor and drinking a kind of soup reinforced by raksi we reached the village. The dwellings were all buried under several feet of snow and I was led to the hut of a man reputed to have a radio. He welcomed me enthusiastically . I was an event in his life, which was understandable when you are buried under six feet of snow for six months of the year. His English was just sufficient to communicate and he then said he would boil some water for the tin hot water bottle which he produced. I thought this was very civil of him but said I was ok and warm enough. No, he explained, it was to warm the world war II radio in the hope that he could contact the military airbase at Leh so that they could pull me out.

Unbelievably, and to my relief, he did contact them and I was instructed to clear a bit of snow and be ready to be picked up and off in minutes. Every day I would pack my ruck sack and clear a trample a circle of snow about 30 yards across. It was depressing living in a tiny room with a single stove which just about prevented me from freezing to death. I would crawl in to my sleeping bag and try reading my book for a second time, but it was not a success. Every afternoon there was a thumping sound from the room next to me, it did not make sense to chop wood inside the building so when there was nobody about I crept in to the next room. To my surprise there was a huge, frozen very dead yak inside. It was complete with fur, legs, hooves, head....... in fact only short of one leg that had been hacked off. This obviously had been my supper, together with some millet, and would have to last until spring if I was not picked up.

After three days I went outside to clear my landing patch with my ruck sack packed and ready when I heard a sound – was it a helicopter? No, yes…. my joy was unbelievable…. I put on my rucksack and ran around my landing patch waving like a mad man. Although I could not see the helicopter I could hear it. Then the helicopter came in to sight – could he see me? Yes, he was coming in to land. It was one of the happiest moments of my life when he landed and I threw my rucksack in to the helicopter and leapt in to the single passenger seat and we were off. The window in the unpredictable Himalayan weather had allowed them to pull me out. We flew back down the spectacular gorge and towards the end spotted my friend who was nearly at the road.

On landing I was taken to the commanding officer who spoke impeccable English and had been to school in England. We had tea together and I often wonder if I had not been English whether I would still be up there eating the rest of the yak. We managed to fly out a week later and eventually returned to England. Then, getting older and perhaps wiser, I decided that this would be my last extreme expedition. Twenty years later I hear that there are now some organized trips going up this river, showing how, like Everest, some of these areas have become more accessible.

CHAPTER 10

Summer Expeditions

During the ten years of mountaineering I interspersed demanding expeditions with less physically challenging ones. This kept me fit and led to interesting ventures.

One of my favourite trips was to Crete in the spring before it became too hot. The plan was to fly in and back pack following vague paths around the east of the island. During such trips there were two memorable incidents. The first when back packing on a very hot day I studied my map and located a sandy beach where I planned to swim and rest. On arrival I found to my dismay that it was a nudist beach. What was I to do? I could keep going, I could wear my bathing trunks, or I could strip off and join the others. I opted for the last and after a swim lay on the beach and fell asleep. What I had forgotten was that I was exposing parts which had never seen the sun before. I got away with just a very red posterior. I should have thought things through and not been distracted by an attractive naked lady.

My second Cretan adventure was very different. I back packed into a remote village a little way inland and realized when I went in to the local bar that it was the Cretan Easter. I was generously offered painted boiled eggs to eat. On leaving the bar I followed a track out of the village to be beckoned in to a garden where they were roasting a whole goat over an open fire.

Appreciating that it was the custom to invite a stranger to join the group and not let them pass the gate, I accepted their hospitality. I was quickly asked if I was German, when I said I was English all was well.

After sampling the roasted goat and red wine an old man, obviously the patriarch of the family, disappeared in to the house to reappear with something wrapped in an oily rag. There were two Mauser pistols and ammunition. With a little difficulty I was able to piece together a remarkable story. During World War II the Germans over ran Crete; there were resistance groups in the mountains and with the aid of the British the partisans captured the German General in command of the island and transported him by submarine in to captivity. This daring feat was the subject of films and the book *Ill Met by Moonlight.*

As reprisals the Germans went in to the villages and killed everybody, men, women and children, shooting and bayoneting them. The old man it seems was left for dead and he insisted on showing me the scars on his rib cage and a bullet wound scar on his arm. I am still not sure what would have happened to me had I been a German!

Other summer time excursions were to the Maritime Alps, the Pecos mountains, Turkey and Greece. The shorter Birmingham University fell walking and mountaineering society trips kept me busy and fit for much of they intervening periods.

Some 30 years later I was in my local pub when the landlord said they were going to enter a team in the Birmingham to Oxford charity bike ride and in view of my stories of my youthful prowess I should join them. Probably, slightly under the influence a couple of pints, I said if I could borrow suitable bike I would join the other three. I managed to find a reasonable bike a few days before the event. Bearing in mind I had not been on a bike for years I was surprised, on taking it around the lanes, how it all came back to me.

On the day of the event we all set off and my team mates disappeared at speed. I had walked the Malvern marathon of 35 miles a few weeks previously and although I finished within the 12 hours I had started too fast and had had cramp. I was not going to get caught twice. However on the other side of Stratford-upon-Avon I was feeling good and decided to chase the others. We all had white racing vests with the name of the pub on the back. I would see a white jersey in front of me but when I caught them it was not one of our team. This went on and I continued to catch people but was exasperated to find they were not one of us. They must be fitter than I thought, was my conclusion.

About five miles from the Oxford finish I saw our support vehicle and trailer which was to take us home at the side of the road. I stopped and expressed my surprise at the performance of the others. Our driver said, what do you mean? they are miles back, they stopped at a feeding station. I was almost an hour in front of the others. Undaunted I pushed hard for the remaining few miles and the pub was phoned to the delight of the drinkers!

This renewed my interest in cycling although at this time my main passion was walking and mountaineering. I decided that road riding was too dangerous and the roads too busy. So I bought myself an off road bike. Off road appealed to me and with friends we completed numerous tracks around the countryside, including completing a set of 25 Cotswold routes. On several occasions I planned a mountain bike route from Bath to Berkswell with a couple of bed and breakfast stops. The idea was to keep tarmac roads to an absolute minimum which meant using bridle and old canal paths and disused railway tracks

In addition to these UK bike rides some overseas trips appealed to me. I joined organized mountain bike groups in South Africa, Pecos mountains and Andalusia in Spain, and another trip in Morocco. The last was interesting because my booking form was returned with a polite letter saying that they thought that the off road route would be too tough for somebody of my age. Disappointed I rang the group leader who before I could discuss the matter said he would be glad to have me with the group – he had spoken to someone who knew me. At the end of the trip the leader said he noticed I was never last up or down hill, whatever the terrain. It was tough and challenging. One broken collar bone and severe bruising (not me!). One of the younger members of the group was particularly complimentary, saying he suddenly saw a shadow behind him on a long climb, he said it was Bill and that I had overtaken him as if it was on the flat. From that day, he said, he was going to give up smoking

A rather adventurous trip which I undertook on my own was to Zanzibar. On arrival I cycled up the coast and stopped at a small hotel. When I explained to the owner that my intention was to cycle across the island to the east coast he looked alarmed. He said, "Don't do that boss, the people in the middle of the island are bad with big knives."

This proved to be good advice and I was able to get a lift in a pick up truck to the extensive sands on the other side of the island. The sands were remarkably firm and I was able to speed along the coast stopping at small beach hotels. Zanzibar was very hot and un-cyclable after 10am; relatively undeveloped it was an exceptional trip.

Fuerta Ventura, the island off the west coast of Africa which is part of the Canaries, was a place I visited several times in winter in search of some sun. During these visits I had become aware that whilst one side of the island had roads, hotels, houses, the other coast appeared to be virtually deserted and as such would be a mountain bike challenge. I recruited two of my friends to join me, explaining that we would be sleeping rough and we would need two water bottles on their bikes because water would not be guaranteed. There was another problem, the only maps easily available were tourist motoring maps. However I did get some military maps which were better than nothing.

Off we went cycling on roads to the north end of the island from where we commenced our off road adventure. The terrain varied from volcanic ash to unrideable rocky surfaces. Occasionally there were beautiful sandy beaches, quite deserted. All went well for a start. Then we came to a series of deep gorges which we could only negotiate by climbing down and then lowering the bikes, then climbing out the other side by a similar method. This was a time consuming process but we kept going, sleeping rough, but occasionally going inland to find a village.

One night when we went inland we found a small bar where we were able to get food and drink. When we emerged it was dark so we agreed if we could find a suitable spot that is where we would sleep This we did and were just settling down when suddenly we were illuminated by car head lights and two men coming towards us. My friends always thought the worst but I went towards the men and shook hands. A technique I had found useful where ever I went. The men went on to explain in broken English that we were camped on a river bed and that if there was one of the frequent storms in the mountains we would be swept away.

After about 10 days off road we reached the end of the island and were back to civilization.

Another unpredictable adventure was when I was boating between the Greek islands. Here I met a Canadian who said he would like to come with me to climb the highest mountain in the Mediterranean islands. Together with the aid of a compass and crude maps we traversed some minor mountains and off road routes. When I said in the course of conversation that I liked fishing he invited me to come to Canada for a week's fishing.

To my surprise he wrote to me a couple of months later saying fly in to Saskatoon in mid Canada and we would go fishing for a week. I wrote back quickly, booked a flight and was met at the airport by a pick up truck full of fishing gear. We were off, driving north for 300 miles on a dirt road which only existed because there was an uranium mine somewhere in the middle of the bush. We stopped the night in a hut at a small Indian settlement and from there it transpired we were to paddle a canoe down river and overland to a remote lake. It was a huge stretch of water several miles long; he had built a hut on an island. Our equipment included a big frying pan and a great hunk of lard, and not much else. During the drive down I had seen huge bears on the side of the road. When I asked whether they were dangerous he said yes. We set off down the river and I was in the front of the canoe; my instructions were to do nothing but paddle like hell when instructed left or right. The river was fast flowing seemingly straight forward until we came round a bend and were faced with rocks and a churning river. Left, right came the instructions which I followed exactly and we survived. After several hours we arrived at a large tranquil lake. We paddled for several hours more to the far end where it was explained that we had reached a portage point. We had to carry the canoe and equipment overland to the next lake. My friend was to carry the canoe on his back and I would carry the food and fishing tackle. Off we went following an ill defined track. After a short time I came to a pile of dung. My instinctive reaction was fancy letting your dog do that in the middle of a path, to be followed quickly by the realization to my horror that it was bear dung. Not only that but it was steaming. My friend was some way back coming along like a giant tortoise so I started to sing *All things Bright and Beautiful*. In retrospect I could not have chosen a more appropriate song. Eventually I reached the lake and to my relief was joined by my friend. He said he had heard me singing and I explained my joy in getting to the lake, saying I could always jump in the lake if the bear came after me. Don't kid yourself, he said, they can swim faster than you.

BEARS

We paddled across to a small island where he had built a hut. We spent the week catching lake trout (the record is 100lba) and living off fish. A splendid adventure where I was embarrassed at not being able to contribute anything towards the costs. My friend however was delighted later with a replica trout which I had carved out of wood and managed to post over.

The day I returned from Canada the phone rang and it was a New Zealander I had met on one of my Mediterranean boat trips. Jill was in England where she had been looking after her daughter's Olympic horses and was now on her way home. This was to change my life although I did not realize it at the time! We got on very well and I was invited to visit New Zealand.

Examining the catch

On arrival in New Zealand Jill met me at Auckland airport and we toured the North Island, staying for a while at Jill's place at Oakura, a beautiful place lying between the sea and snow capped Mt Taranaki. Jill's good friend's husband was also a keen fisherman. He took me in his boat out from New Plymouth where we caught a number of bottom feeding fish before locating a shoal of tuna. These were tremendous sport but although I had a strap around my waist I had to give up after catching three. On our return the tuna were quickly barbecued and, with a slice of lime, were perhaps the finest fish I have ever tasted.

David also invited me to join an all male camping party who took their boats annually to Lake Waekaremoana for a week. The lake was huge and remote and we set up our wild camp there amid the native bush. I was told that all would be provided but that I needed to get some wet artificial flies. The fishing shop could not give me any recommendations so I settled on half a dozen "grenadiers", a red and black wet fly. Luck was with me, despite looking like a bit of rag in the water it was very successful and I finished giving some of my flies to others in the party. Beginners luck?!

Fishing New Zealand's Lake Waekaremoana a week in the bush with the men.

The many trout we caught were smoked on an

improvised under ground smoker which was the first thing we built after erecting the tents. I was unable to contribute in any way but on return I made a replica five pound brown trout in a glass case and sent it back to New Zealand. On seeing it, a visitor and

Back in England I carved replicas of the trout we caught.

knowledgeable fisherman to my friend, said "don't tell

me I will tell you which lake that trout was caught". He was a little surprised when he learnt it was made out of wood.

Another most enjoyable experience for me was a fortnight spent with Jill's sister and brother-in-law who had retired from farming and lived on a yacht. Based in the Bay of Islands, the fishing was superb, and we caught all kinds of fish using a variety of techniques. Sometimes baiting three hooks on one line and catching three different species of fish, including snapper a favourite for eating. The biggest fish we caught was nine foot hammer head shark which we brought alongside the boat to remove the hooks before releasing it.

A fishing technique that was used was to have rods in sockets at the back of the boat with tassel type lures. I was surprised that fish took the lures when we were travelling at such high speed. I had taken some English pike lures with me and when I suggested we try them they laughed but agreed. The surface pike lures proved to be effective even though they kept breaking the surface and I caught more on my lures than the more conventional ones they had provided.

There were often too many fish and we would stop fishing. This frequently occurred when we spotted great numbers of seagulls whirling around in a small area. If we circled the boat around the area of activity we would catch the predatory fish, mainly kahawai which had rounded up a shoal of small fish and there was a feeding frenzy. All that was needed was a small red wet fly which obviously represented bloody fragments of small fish.

We visited New Zealand several times. Once we were lent a camper van which allowed us to visit some remote areas and provided me with some more excellent fishing in the far north and on the Coromandel. I was very surprised how sea fishing in shallow surf yielded such big fish.

In 2004 we got married and Jill came to live permanently in England. Jill, who although a very competent horse woman, was not a cyclist. However she took to cycling as they say like to duck to water, round England and numerous European trips, mainly in France. We mountain biked on different occasions around Nice, Brittany and the Loire, always taking our chances on finding places to stay; Jill's good French, better than mine, proved a real advantage.

Still mountain biking at 85, but more slowly, we rode 20

miles around Rutland water a few weeks ago in rather adverse wet and windy weather. We also spent a pleasant week, cycling round the Ile de Re.

Lightning Source UK Ltd.
Milton Keynes UK
UKOW06f2234130515

251490UK00006B/54/P